* 1,000,000 *

Free E-Books
@
www.ForgottenBooks.org

* Alchemy *

The Secret is Revealed
@
www.TheBookofAquarius.com

Forgotten Books

Hundreds of Things a Boy Can Make

A Hobby Book for Boys of All Ages

By

Unknown Author

Published by Forgotten Books 2012

PIBN 1000025308

Copyright © 2012 Forgotten Books
www.forgottenbooks.org

Hundreds of Things A Boy Can Make

A HOBBY BOOK FOR BOYS OF ALL AGES

LONDON
W. FOULSHAM & CO., LTD.

BOOK PRODUCTION WAR ECONOMY STANDARD

THIS BOOK IS PRODUCED IN COMPLETE CONFORMITY WITH THE AUTHORIZED ECONOMY STANDARDS.

Made in Great Britain
BY C. TINLING & CO., LTD., LIVERPOOL LONDON AND PRESCOT.
COPYRIGHT: W. FOULSHAM & CO., LTD.

PREFACE

There is a great deal in this book to attract and interest the average healthy-minded boy. With a copy of it at his elbow, he will always be able to spend his time profitably and he will never be at a loss to know how to while away an hour or so pleasantly.

Probably no book of its kind has been packed with so much useful matter as is contained within the present covers. There are innumerable paragraphs describing the making of toys, suitable for his own use as well as that of his boy and girl friends; there are directions on the construction of useful articles for the home; there are detailed descriptions of things to make for bazaars and sales of work; and there are dozens of brilliant ideas that will keep him busy and amused for hours.

It is not a book that, once read, possesses no further interest; it is a guide and reference that will be turned to on a thousand occasions.

1057599

CONTENTS

	PAGE		PAGE
Aerial Ropeway, An	26	" Counting Out "	101
Air Pressure Experiment, An	70	Crane, A Working	48
All in a Row	111	Crazy Path in the Garden, Making a	19
Aquarium, A Home-made	42		
At Your Service, Mr. Smoker	98	Cricket Score Board, A	49
Ball for Windy Weather, A	33	Crystal Bells	37
Barometer, A Boy's	34	Curing an Animal's Skin	88
Bird in the Hand, The	41	Cut-out Designs	109
Bird Table, Making a	31	Dancing Darkie, The	143
Blowing Up Your Football	32	Dart Board, A	59
Boat Driven By Air, A	11	Defying Gravity	9
Book Ends, A Pair of	84	Desk For Your Den, A	81
Book Ends, Another Idea for	85	Dog Fight, The	151
Bookplate, Make Your Own	83	Door, Making a	54
Boomerang That is Different, The	41	Draught Screen, A Modernistic	80
		Dummy Black-lead, A	145
Bow and Arrow, A	67	Electric Bell, An	71
Broom for the Garden, A	25	Electric Burglar Alarm, An	73
Broom Rack, A	68	Electric Light Shade, An Inverted	75
Buffer Stop, A Spring	121		
Camp Fires, For	19	Escalator, An Easily-made	155
Camp Stool, Making a	18	Expanding Toy, An	69
Can You See Through a Brick?	106	Feather Glider, A	17
Cannon that Can be Fired, A	157	Fish Globe, The	140
Capacious Wine Bottle, The	153	Flower Bed, A Novel	21
Cinder Sifter, A	12	Fretwork Articles to Make	90
Cinema, Your Own	102	Fretwork, Making Things in	88
Climbing Monkey, The	93	Fun in the Aquarium	12
Coat Hanger in the Scullery, A	77	Funny Faces	149
Collecting-Box, Making a	112	Goggles	148
Copper Name-plate for the House, A	22	Goldfish and Globe, The	139
		Hard Labour	94
Copying Apparatus, A Useful	86	Hat Stand, A	86
Corks, The Game of	130	Helicopter, A Flying	29

Contents

	PAGE		PAGE
Helicopter, Another	30	Musical Box, A	131
He Wags His Tail	92	Musical Glasses	150
Iron Expands When Heated, To Prove That	67	Musical Windmill, The	158
		Music Hath Charms	136
Is it Going to Rain?	33	Nesting Boxes	21
Jigsaw Puzzles, An Idea for	107	Noisy Rattle, A	138
Jolly Anglers, The	39	Numbered Board, The	58
Keeping Weekly Periodicals Tidy	9	Optical Illusions, Making	144
		Ornamenting a Clothes-brush	79
Kiddie's Seat Scooter, A	51	Paper Shape of Five Squares, The	110
Kite for Windy Weather, A	29		
Ladder, Making a	23	Papier Maché Models, Making	108
Lifebuoy, A	65	Parachute, An Easily Made	24
Magic Inks	106	Pea-Shooter, A Home-made	151
Magic Tops, Six	36	Periscope, A Cheap	59
Magnifying Glass, A Home-made	105	Perpetual Motion—Almost	113
		Pipe Rack, A	105
Marble Board, A	141	Poison Bottles Safe, Making the	76
Marketing Board, A	74	Poles for Net-Ball	39
Marking Out Tennis, Football and Other Pitches	14	Polishing the Wooden Articles You Construct	96
Matchbox Holder, A	10	Printing a Poster	101
Model Aeroplane, A	27	Puzzle, A Capital	11
Model Railway Accessories, Six—		Rack, A Handy	82
Loading Gauge, A	116	Railroad Track	120
Telegraph Posts	117	Railway Trains Easily Made, Jolly	115
Gradient Posts	117		
Buffer Stops	118	Railway Tunnel, A	119
Field Hoardings	118	Re-Enamelling Your Cycle	43
Bridge, An Easily Made	118	Revolving Cardboard Toy, A	146
Model Railway Bookstall, A	118	Rings, Amusing	153
Models Made of Cement	159	Rocking Nigger, The	137
Model Town Accessories, Six—		Roving Eyes, Those	147
Pillar-Boxes	141	Rubber Stamp With Your Initials, A	86
Sign Posts	142		
Motor Sign Posts	143	Sack Mystery, The	151
Automatic Machines	143	Saucepan Holder for Campers, A	15
Rustic Fences	143	Scooter, Making a	49
Bus and Tram Stops	143	Seat for Campers, A Comfortable	16
Motor Bus, Lighting Up a	132		
Motor Car Number Plates	45	See-Saw, A	57
Motor Horn, Your	46	Shadow Theatre, Comical	114

Contents

	PAGE	
Ship, A Self-propelled	65	Toy Engine, A
Shunting the Trucks	122	Toy Fort, A
Smoke Rings, Beautiful	100	Toy Lawn Roller, A
Snake in the Box, The	134	Toy Windmill, A
Snake, The Realistic	16	" T " Puzzle, A
Spider's Web, Catching a	20	Train Indicator, A
Splendid Catch, A	13	Trimming Device for Snapshots, A
Stamp Collection, Making an Interesting	100	Trouser Hanger Made of Clothes Pegs, A
Stilts, A Pair of	52	
Sturdy Steed, The	61	Try Your Skill
Such a Commotion !	13	Union Jack, Making a
Swat that Fly	69	Useful Gadget, A
Table Skittles	97	Violin Out of a Cigar Box, How to Make a
Telephone, Your	154	
Things You Can Easily Make for Christmas and Birthday Presents; Also To Sell at Bazaars	123	Walking-Stick, Making a
		Waste-Paper Basket, A Strong
		Water Cutter, The
Tie Press, A Useful	78	Water From Nowhere
Tinting Electric Light Bulbs	113	Waterproofing Matches
Tip Waggon, A Wooden	46	What a Clatter !
Tivoli Board, A	103	What Does Your Voice Look Like ?
Toboggan You Can Make, A	54	
Top That Spins in the Air, A	35	Whirling Toy, The
Towel Rack, A Fancy	87	Winder for Model Aeroplanes,
Toy Calendars	97	Woman Who Walks, The
Toy Chest, A	130	? ? ?

Hundreds of Things A Boy Can Make

KEEPING WEEKLY PERIODICALS TIDY

Probably you buy a boy's paper every week and, though you may not wish to have the copies bound, you may like to keep them for reference. If so, stack up the parts in their proper order and then, thread a piece of tape through the wire stitches, as shown in the larger illustration. The small, right-hand sketch shows the thickness of a part with one of the wire stitches and the tape passed under it.

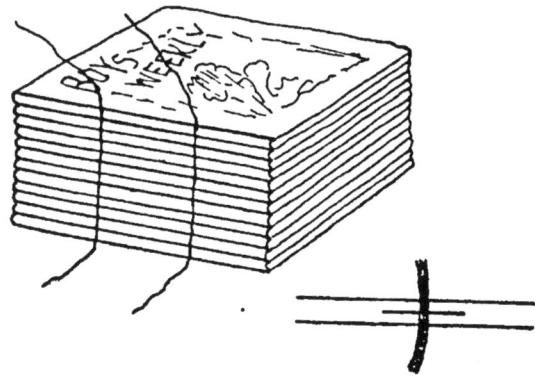

When the stack is made tie the two ends of the tape in a bow, so that it can be easily undone next week when the subsequent part is to be added to the stack. It is a good idea to paste a sheet of brown paper along the edge of the top copy to serve as cover and keep the first part clean.

DEFYING GRAVITY

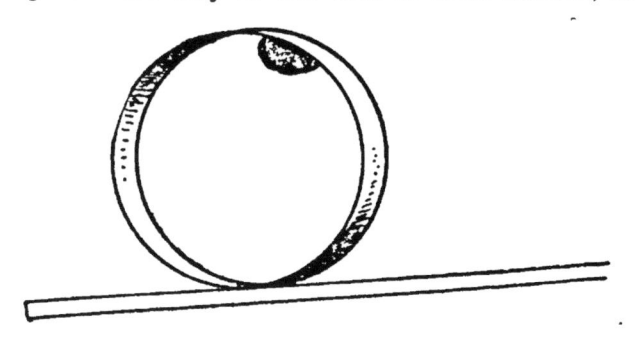

Get a round cardboard tube, such as people use for sending things through the post which they do not wish to have creased, and cut an inch off it, either with a fretsaw or a pocket-knife. Be careful that in doing this you do not flatten any part of the circumference, because it must be a perfect ring. Then stick a big dab of plasticene on it, as shown in the diagram.

Now stand the ring on a slightly inclined plane and it will roll slowly uphill, thus defying gravity. The dab of material, stuck on the inner face of the ring, must be placed at the top, just a trifle towards the uphill direction, when starting.

A MATCHBOX HOLDER

The accompanying sketch shows an easily made matchbox holder. The wooden base consists of an odd piece of thin material left over from some other job. It should be about 7 by 3 inches. When the edges have been nicely trimmed up and smoothed, the metal tray is added.

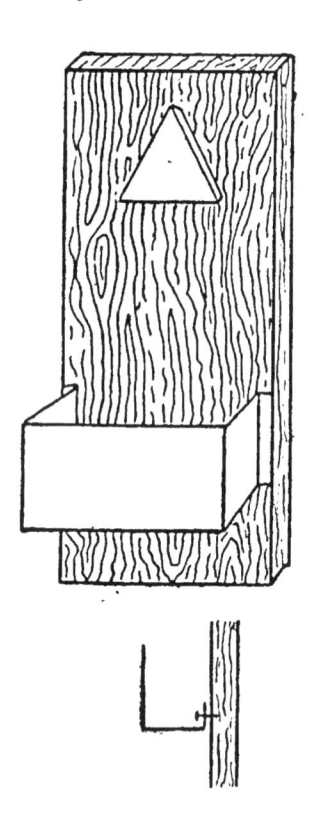

The larger sketch shows how the sides are shaped whilst the smaller one explains how the bottom is fixed to the base. For metal, a piece of sheet brass or copper is best, though an empty tin, flattened out, will serve well enough, if given a coat of enamel. File the edges to make them quite smooth. A raised triangle has been added, in the present case, by way of ornamentation, but a dozen other forms of decoration will occur to any handy boy. Stain and polish the wood or give it two coats of some bright enamel.

A CAPITAL PUZZLE

Take two thin pieces of wood, of the size shown by the square. With your fretwork saw, cut out, from one of them, the X-shaped pattern, and glue the piece surrounding the X to the untouched square. Then, get four tiny ball-bearing balls from the nearest cycle shop. They should be less

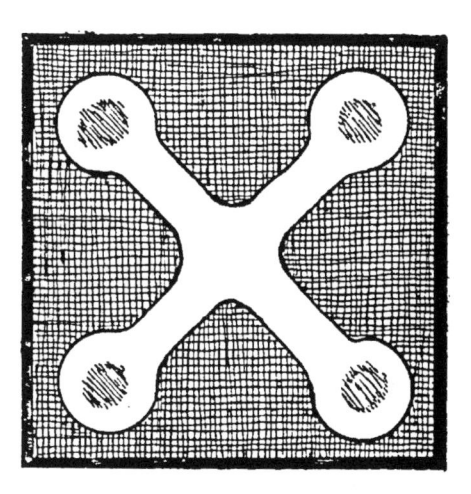

in diameter than the thickness of the wood. Countersink a shallow depression at the centre of each of the four circles. Drop the four balls in the channels, add a square of glass to fit over the wood and bind up the edges with passe-partout strips.

You now have an admirable puzzle. The game is to get all the four balls, at the same time, in the depressions within the small circles.

A BOAT DRIVEN BY AIR

If you are one of those boys who like to experiment with things, here is something that will amuse you.

Get a lightly built model rowing boat and put a small length of metal tubing through the stern end, so that it projects under water. Then

12 Hundreds of Things a Boy Can Make

blow up an air balloon and close the neck by means of a wire clip. Fit the end of the neck to the inner end of the tube and tie it on securely. The balloon now lies in the boat and must be fastened down to prevent it blowing up.

Now put the boat in water, release the wire clip and the escaping air will drive it along.

A CINDER SIFTER

This is an article which will save a good deal of money in the fuel bill. The easiest way to make it is to get a stout wooden box, with an opening a trifle larger than the sieve which is used in the kitchen, to knock out

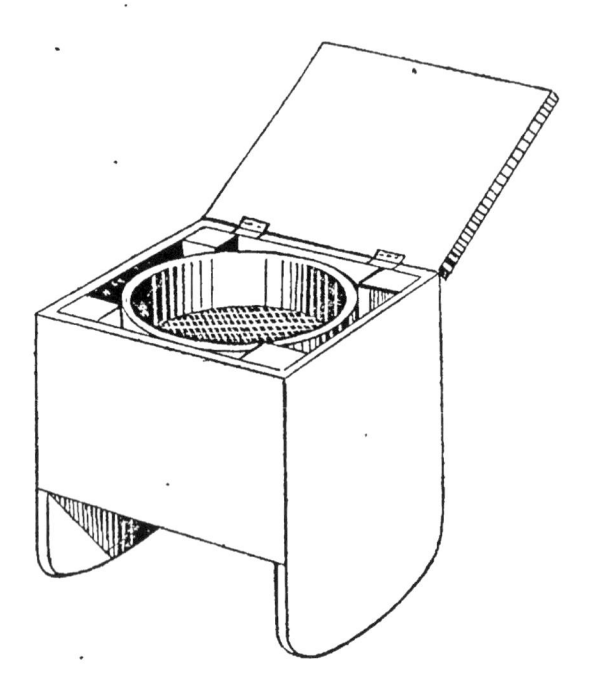

the bottom and cut off the lower part of the back and front. Then, the sides are trimmed to a curve, so that they may serve as the necessary rockers. Nail two ledges of wood on the inside for supporting the sieve and fit a piece of wood, by means of two hinges, to act as a lid. Then this very useful article is finished.

FUN IN THE AQUARIUM

Place two aquaria side by side, as shown in the diagram, and stock one of them plentifully with tadpoles. Then procure a length of glass tubing of stout bore and bend it to form a sort of bridge, as the one depicted in the picture. The tubing can be bent by heating it in a Bunsen flame and then pressing it as required. Place the tube under a tap of water and thus fill it. Close both its outlets with your hands and stand it in the aquaria as shown. The water will remain in the tube if the ends were plunged under the surface before you removed your hands.

Hundreds of Things a Boy Can Make

With the bridge full of water, the tadpoles will dart up it and travel to the second tank. In fact, they will be making the journey, one way or the other, without ceasing.

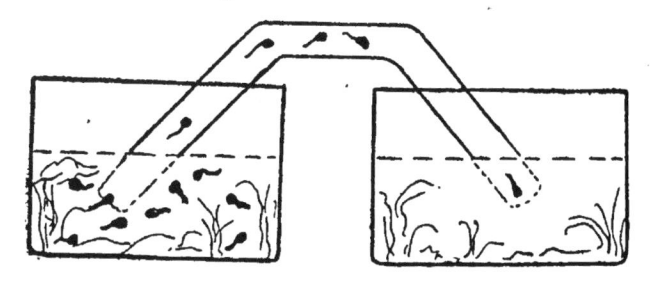

If you keep goldfish, you can make a bridge for them, too, but the tube will have to be considerably wider than for tadpoles.

A SPLENDID CATCH

If you have a fret-saw, cut out the letters forming the word *last*, adhering as much as possible to the shapes of the letters shown in the diagram. Use thin wood for the purpose.

Then, set out the letters as we have given them and ask your friends to change *last* into *first*. They can employ any method they like as long as they do not want to use anything beyond the four pieces you have set before them.

It is only rarely that anyone spots the solution; it is merely to leave out the letter *a*. Without this letter, you have *1st*.

SUCH A COMMOTION !

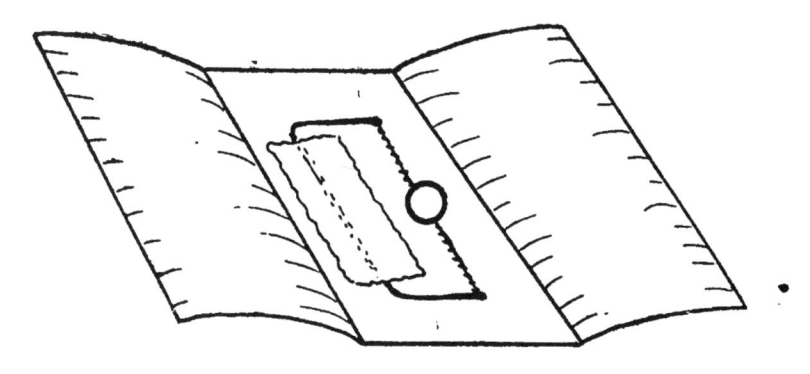

If you would like to play a trick on a friend, send him one of these contrivances in an envelope. It consists of a stout card, folded into three. To the card is fixed a U-shaped piece of wire, held firmly in position by means of a gummed label. At each end of the wire is an elastic band which, together, grip a ring made of wire or any light metal.

When all is ready, twist the ring over about twenty times and so knot up the rubber bands. Then, carefully fold over the two flaps of card, without letting the ring uncoil, and slip the uncanny thing into the envelope.

Your friend receives the letter, tears it open, pulls out the card and to his horror the ring uncoils itself. It will give him the fright of his life.

A USEFUL GADGET

This gadget has dozens of uses. It will be invaluable if you do leather-work and have to prick a number of spaces all equidistant, say when thonging. It will come in handy when you have to rule a number of lines with equal spaces between them. And, it would be easy to suggest a score of other uses.

This is how it is made. Take a cog-wheel from an old alarm clock or even from a watch that has ceased to function, fit a short piece of wire through the axis, slip a tiny washer on each side and, then, fix on two thin pieces of wood to serve as a handle. Bind them together with fine wire, but do not approach too close to the wheel or it will refuse to rotate freely.

MARKING OUT TENNIS, FOOTBALL AND OTHER PITCHES

It is a very tedious job to mark out tennis courts and football pitches if you do not possess an expensive machine for the purpose and you employ the ordinary hand method. The white lines can be made easily and well, however, if you construct a board like that shown in the illustration. It consists of two long strips of three-ply wood, with a space of 2 inches separating them.

All you do is to put the board down on the ground where the white line is to come and, then, you brush the whitewash on the grass seen through the opening. When one length is done, the board is lifted and

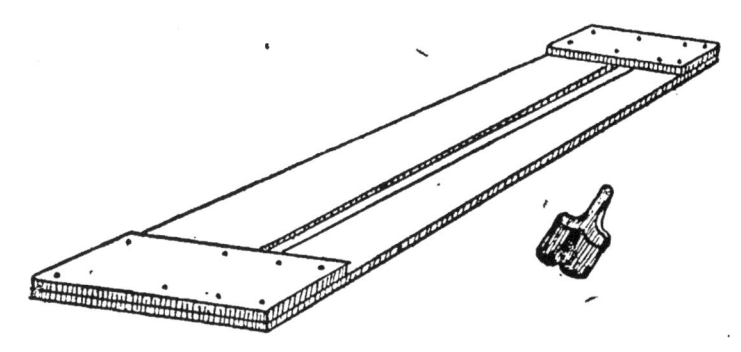

placed in position for the next length. And so on, until all the lines are completed.

Give an eye to the underface of the contrivance and wipe it if any of the wash creeps on to it.

A SAUCEPAN HOLDER FOR CAMPERS

Don't burn your fingers any more when lifting a can of boiling liquid from the camp fire. Cut a fork of the shape shown in the illustration from a bush or tree. Note the notch indicated by the arrow. When you want to lift a can from the fire and pour out its contents, slip the

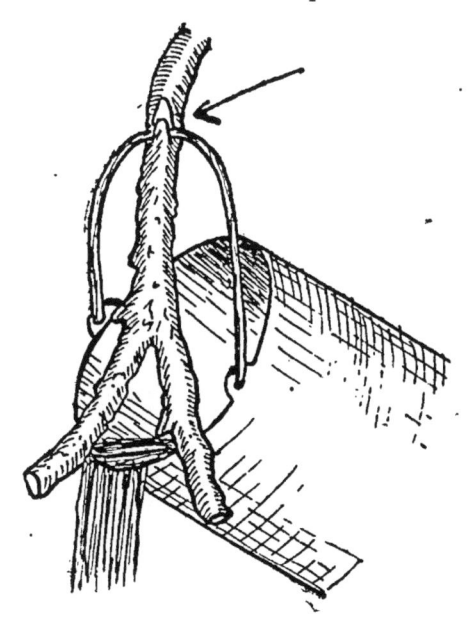

handle into the notch and the prongs of the Y will help you to tilt out the liquid.

Be quite certain that your wood is sound and that it will not snap.

A COMFORTABLE SEAT FOR CAMPERS

Nobody expects camp-life to be as comfortable as things are at home ; but we have often felt, when camping, that a nice springy seat would be a pleasant change to the hard unyielding ground.

If you want to fit up a comfortable camp seat, take three stout poles—Scouts will, of course, use their poles—place them in a bundle on the ground and tie them tightly together, about three inches from one end.

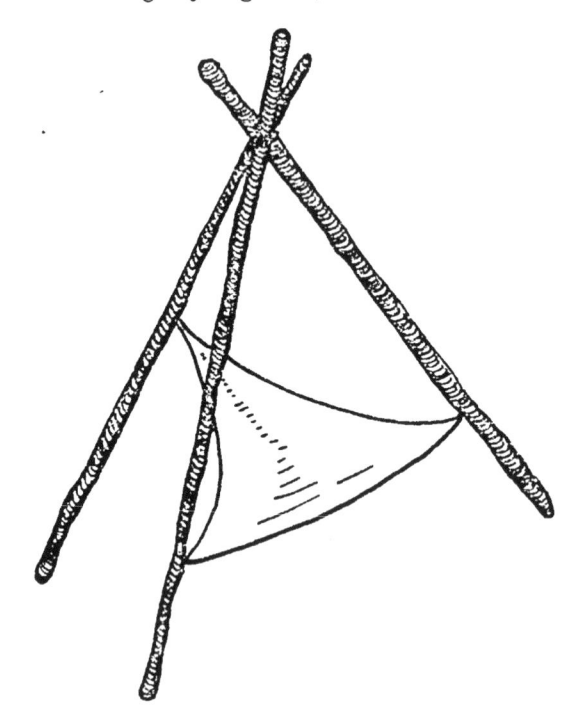

When this is done, lift up one of the poles and revolve it through half a circle, carrying it down to the ground again, but away from the other two. Now raise the three poles, bound ends upwards, spread out the feet and you have a very rigid tripod.

Next, take a ground sheet—the smallest one you have—fold it into a triangle and tie each corner to one of the legs of the tripod, about a foot above the ground. This makes a very comfortable seat.

THE REALISTIC SNAKE

Most people do not like snakes, though the majority of them are quite harmless, and all are scrupulously clean. If you would like to make one that nobody will object to, go out in the autumn and collect from under the oak-trees a handful of acorn cups.

When you have brought them home, grade them according to size—the big ones first and the little ones last. Then bore a hole through each cup, making the perforation at the point where the stalk grows. A fine awl or a packing-case needle will do the work admirably.

Now thread a piece of tough, fine string through the cups, placing them one outside the other, beginning at the largest and working along to the smallest, when the tail is reached. All must be put the same way.

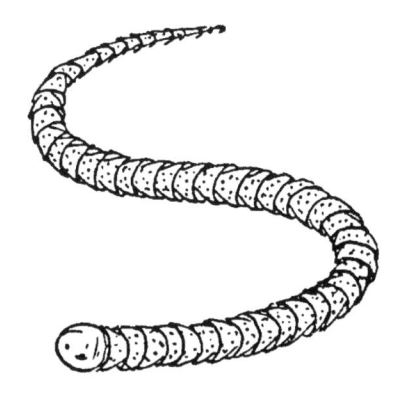

For the snake's head, fit an acorn in the first cup and give it a touch of glue to hold it in position. You now have a creepy-crawly snake with a spotted back and, if you draw a face on the acorn, with a very lifelike appearance.

A FEATHER GLIDER

Some boys are never so happy as when they are devising gliders and flying them. A good many ingenious patterns have been thought out, and the one described here is as good as any we have seen.

Take a piece of cane about eight inches long and to each end fit a cork, holding it in position by means of a dab of sealing-wax. One cork should be about twice as heavy as the other. Next get four feathers, two fairly large and two much smaller. Force the points of the larger ones into the heavier cork and those of the smaller feathers into the lighter cork. See that all the four feathers lie in the same plane, or, if preferred, tilt them up a little to that the front edge is lower than the back edge. Then dab some more sealing-wax on the points to hold them firmly in the corks. A splendid glider is the result.

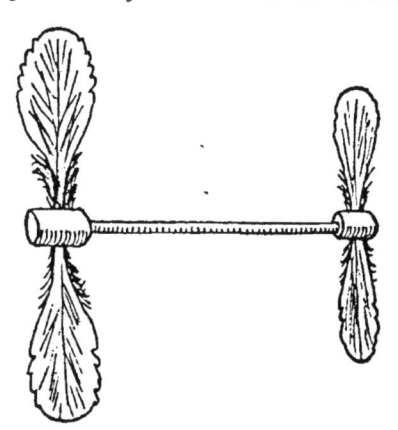

B

MAKING A CAMP STOOL

Camp stools are useful not only in camps but in the garden, in theatre queues and in dozens of other places. You can make one in an afternoon, for a few pence.

For the job, the following strips of wood are required :

4 lengths, each 20 inches long and one inch in section.
2 lengths, each 12 inches long and one inch in section.
2 stout dowel rods, each about ten inches long. (A dowel rod is a strip of wood, circular in section.)

The wood is put together so as to make two frames, as shown in the lower sketch. At the top is a 12 inch length ; at the sides, two 20 inch strips and, joining these, down below, is a dowel rod.

When the two frames are made, one is dropped within the other and then bolted together, at a point a trifle higher than the middle of the length. In order that this may be possible, the two frames must not be made the same width. Make the width between the two uprights of the larger frame, eight and three-quarter inches, and the outside width of the smaller frame, a full eighth of an inch less. Then, they will fit nicely.

The two legs are joined to the top rail by cutting them to a slight taper and inserting in holes shaped to take them. They should wedge in tightly and be glued as well.

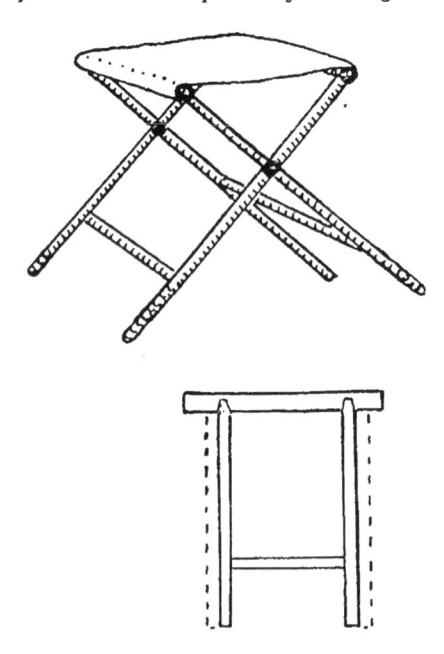

The dowel rods are inserted in holes made with a brace and bit. They, too, should be glued.

Where the two frames are to be bolted together, make a round hole through the two strips, insert a bolt and tighten up by means of a nut. A thin metal washer should be placed between the two pieces of wood.

As the frames have to be hinged in two places, all this has to be done twice.

For the seat part, obtain any suitable piece of stout material, eighteen by twelve inches, fold it along the edges so that it measures eighteen by ten and a half inches, and tack the two short ends to the upper strips of the frame. Place the tacks as far under the strips as they will conveniently go, so that there is no fear of sitting on them.

It is not a bad plan to round all the edges of the wood before it is made up.

FOR CAMP FIRES

All of you who love camping will find this simple piece of apparatus of considerable use. It consists of three long strap hinges, such as can be bought in the multiple stores for 2d. each. Each hinge is bent outwards

to form a right-angle and, then, the three tips are held together by means of a flat bolt. This is arranged over the camp fire, the remaining tips are forced into the ground and you have a rigid support for standing on it such things as kettles and frying-pans. The contrivance will fold up and pack flat when being carried in the kit.

MAKING A CRAZY PATH IN THE GARDEN

A crazy path gives your garden an old-world appearance which is very pleasing. Most people construct such paths out of odd-shaped pieces of flag-stones; but the varying thicknesses of the pieces gives the path an uneven tread, which makes walking not at all easy. In fact, a surface of this character is positively dangerous when youngsters are about.

To construct a safe crazy path, remove the soil to a depth of four inches, then obtain a number of wooden laths, all four inches in width and cut them into varying lengths of from twelve to twenty inches.

Set these laths, on edge, along the two sides of the path, placing them in a slightly irregular manner, i.e. let them wind about somewhat and do not make the path exactly the same width throughout. Then, put in some cross pieces to reach from side to side. These, also, should be fitted in a manner that is devoid of regularity.

When this has been done, make up some concrete; then, having slightly wetted the ground, spread the concrete between the laths and smooth off the surface with a flat piece of lath.

In three or four days' time, pull out the laths which shaped the path and use them for the next strip that is to be constructed. Naturally, you will not attempt the entire run in one day.

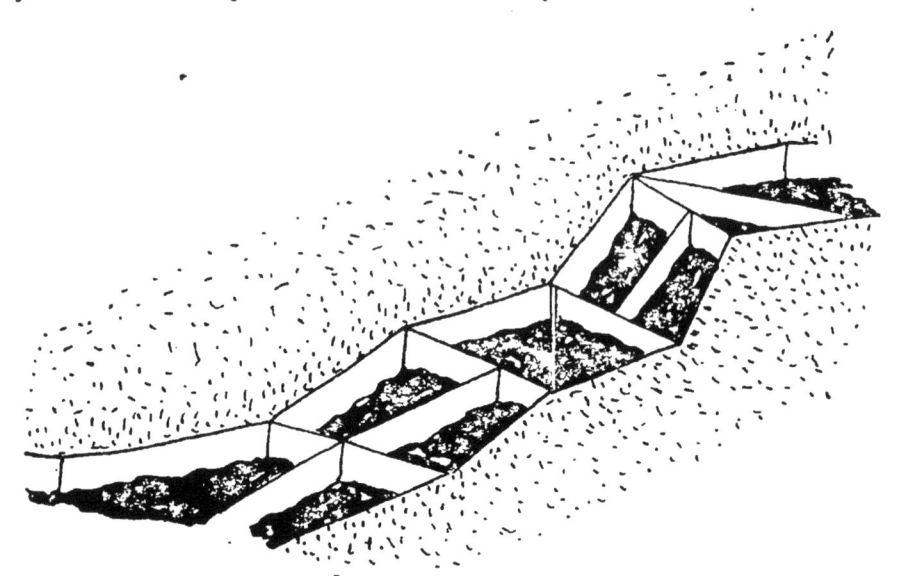

Do not be in a hurry to walk on the path. Allow it two or three weeks to harden, if possible. Then sprinkle earth in the cracks, caused when you removed the laths, and sow grass seed.

The concrete required for this work should be made by mixing one part of Portland cement, two of sharp sand and four of broken material, with sufficient water to make a wet paste. The broken material may consist of stones picked up in the garden, old bricks smashed into small fragments, disused flower pots similarly treated and any suitable material of the same character that happens to be available. The cement and the sand are procured from the local builders' merchant. All the ingredients should be shovelled together on the stone flags in the backyard or on some boards laid together, and, when well mixed, the water is added, a little at a time.

CATCHING A SPIDER'S WEB

Few things are more fragile than a spider's web and most people would think it was nonsense to try and keep one for any length of time. As a matter of fact, we have one that was made last autumn and it is as perfect to-day as it was when the spider wove it.

How did we manage? First, we obtained a sheet of smooth cardboard and, mind, it must be very smooth—quite free from any coarseness. Then, we went over it with Indian ink and made it absolutely black. At this stage, we put the card carefully away and waited for a suitable opportunity.

Early one morning in September, when the weather was still, we got up and looked round the garden. There were several fine spiders' webs to be seen, so we hurried indoors and painted the black card with a thin layer of gum. Without losing any time, we returned to the garden, placed the card under a suitable web and lifted it so that the threads were caught by the gum. A pair of scissors severed the outlying threads and the web was ours.

The gum dried in less than an hour and, then, we covered the card with a clean sheet of glass which was bound up with passe-partout edging.

Don't you think the idea a capital one ?

We should add, perhaps, that webs are a little deceiving in their size. They are larger than they seem, so be provided with a fairly large piece of cardboard or you will miss the outer threads, which are, probably, the most beautiful of all.

A NOVEL FLOWER BED

Have you a pair of old motor-tyre covers that nobody wants ? If so, why not make this novel flower bed with them ? Just drop them down somewhere, one on top of the other, preferably on a stretch of the lawn, up near one corner. Drive four wooden stakes into the ground inside the covers and equidistant, to keep the latter from moving. Then, fill

up with good soil and plant your flowers. Naturally, you can grow anything in this bed—geraniums, pansies and a host of other plants. A good idea would be to push half a dozen stakes into the ground to form a pyramid and plant sweet peas. They would make a lovely show.

NESTING BOXES

Fifteen years ago we built a nesting box and hung it on a tree in a shady spot of the garden where cats could not reach it. During every one of those fifteen years it has been tenanted by blue tits. These feathered visitors have made a welcome addition to the garden, which most of us would appreciate.

should you desire to make a nesting box of this character, obtain a piece of a tree trunk at least a foot and a half long, and no less than three-quarters of a foot in diameter. Then bore out a chamber 9 in. down and 6 in. wide. Do this by burning with a red-hot iron, or by chipping and

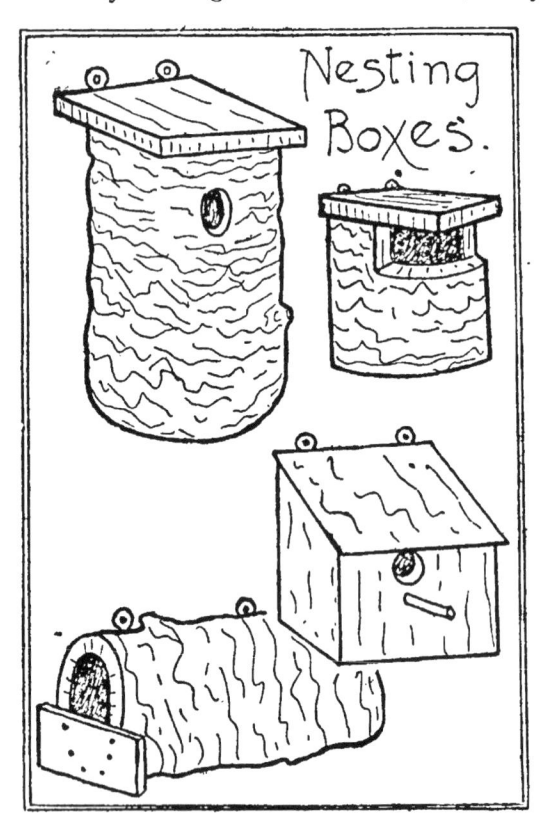

using a drill. Three inches from the top cut a circular hole through the side, 2 in. in diameter, to serve as an entrance. Lastly, nail a piece of wood on the top to take the place of a roof.

Hang up the box some time before the nesting season, in order that its newness may have worn off before the birds wish to take up their residence in it. Also, hang it tilted slightly forward; if it slopes backwards, rain may beat in through the entrance hole. Place it in a shady spot, and never on a wall. The illustration shows four patterns.

A COPPER NAME-PLATE FOR THE HOUSE

You cannot go into a shop and buy a name-plate for fixing to your front gate, and there is a certain amount of difficulty in getting one made specially for you. You can, however, make one yourself, and if you do it to your parents' satisfaction what more could be desired?

You will want, first of all, a strip of sheet copper, about 12 in. by 4 in. Get it fairly thin, though not nearly so thin as the tinned iron that is used for making condensed milk tins. Perhaps it will be as well to tell the man in the shop where you buy it what you want it for, and he will give you the right material.

We said, above, that you will need a strip of copper about 12 in. by 4 in. These are good average dimensions, but before you decide measure up the space where you intend to fix the plate. Perhaps your gate will not take quite such a wide strip.

The next thing to do is to draw your plate, with the appropriate lettering, on a sheet of paper in full scale. You should not try your hand with regular-shaped letters, as the slightest inequality of height or spacing will brand the work as that of an amateur. Rather, go in for fanciful letters, for little defects will then pass off as some smart conceit of yours.

Now transfer the design to the copper, using carbon paper for the purpose, and this done you must chase or cut the pattern into the metal. Nail the strip by the four corners to a flat piece of soft wood, and chase with an old screw-driver, sharpened up to a chisel edge. The chaser is placed on the line that is to be cut with the forward tip of the blade slightly raised. By gently tapping with a hammer it travels along almost without assistance. Be careful not to cut right through the copper.

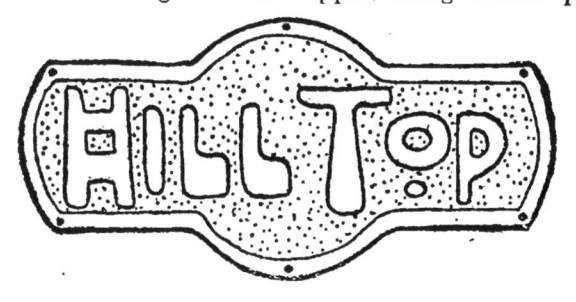

When all the lines are indented turn the plate over, and placing it on an old hassock or thick mat, hollow out the letters. The tool required for this is easily made by filing a short steel rod until it has a domed head. You, of course, hit it with a hammer.

The letters, being hollowed out on the underside, are raised on the upper side. Now we have to put a matt surface all over the background of the design.

A stout French nail, with the point cut off and the stump end filed into cross lines, makes an admirable tool for the purpose. Hammer this tool all over the ground-work and obliterate the pattern of the tool.

The next thing is to cut the edge of the plate with shears, or, if a fanciful edging is desired, with a metal fret-saw. Now polish nicely and the plate is completed.

MAKING A LADDER

Most boys like to make a ladder at some time or other in their careers, and you may be contemplating the construction of one, at the moment. There is nothing difficult about putting a ladder together, if you do not mind it being a trifle heavy.

You will want two pieces of wood, square in section, with two inch sides. The length will depend on the maximum height you wish to climb. Eight feet ought to be about the most. More than this will put a great strain on the wood, and specially chosen materials will be

24 *Hundreds of Things a Boy Can Make*

needed. See that your strips are free from flaws and smooth them properly with glass-paper.

To make the treads, cut strips of wood, each eight inches long. Make them from material, two inches wide and one inch thick.

The next thing is to arrange the two long strips flat on the floor and parallel with each other. Let their outside edges be exactly eight inches apart. Put a mark on the two strips at every ninth inch of the run and, at these points, make a space two inches wide and one inch deep. Cut down the sides of this space with a saw and knock out the unwanted wood with a chisel and mallet. Into these spaces, the treads will fit and there they should be fixed by two long screws at each end.

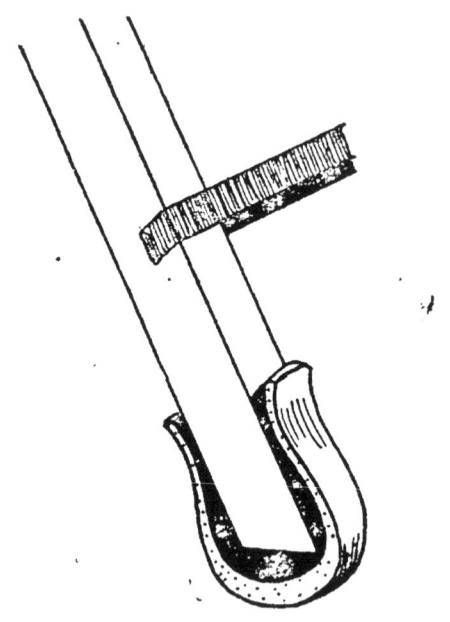

When this is done, it is not a bad idea to round the two upper edges of each tread by means of a spoke-shave. This will give your feet a more convenient purchase.

The job is now finished, but you may like to make yours an extra-special ladder. You know that most ladders have a particularly unpleasant habit of slipping when stood on any smooth surface. To overcome this, get a piece of old motor-tyre, cut off two sections and fix to the feet of the ladder, as shown in the illustration.

AN EASILY MADE PARACHUTE

Great fun can be had by flying a parachute on days when there is a moderate wind. You want to stand on a small hill with the breeze behind you. Be careful when letting the apparatus free that the threads are not entangled and that the paper dome is in proper shape.

To make a good flying parachute, get a sheet of tissue paper and trim it to the shape shown on the next page. The large cut-out section is needed to supply the domed shape of the body. Overlap B on A and the flat piece of tissue immediately becomes conical. Next, bring together the two sides of all the cut-out V's. While together, stick a small patch of paper on each, to keep them in place. At the same time, fit a length of cotton on each flap and the patch will hold it there.

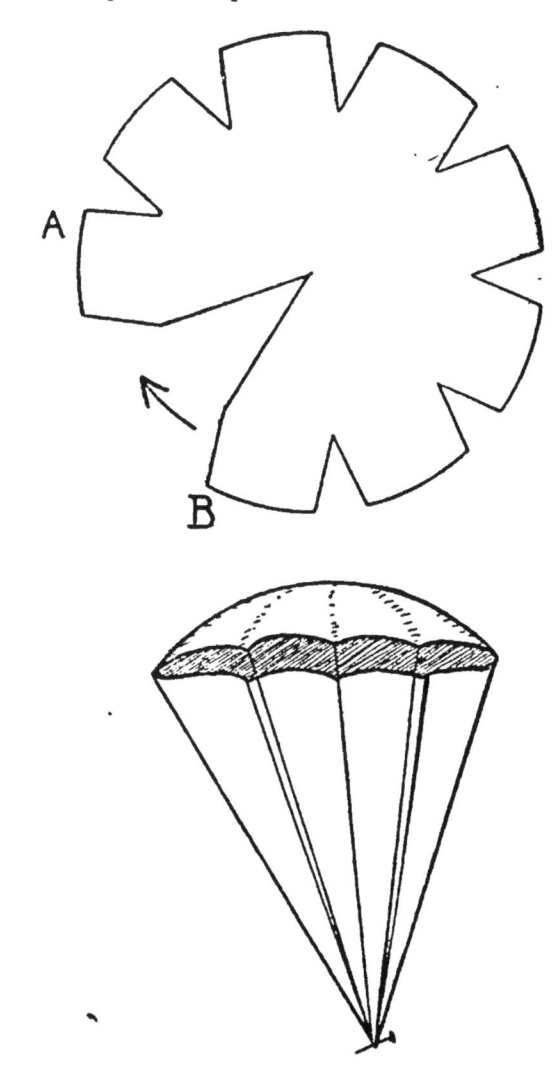

Wait a few hours for the sticking to dry, then trim all the pieces of cotton to the same length, tie them in a knot and fit in the loop, a small nail, to act as balancer.

Do not let a sudden gust of wind tear the fabric, and keep away from the branches of trees.

A BROOM FOR THE GARDEN

Stiff bass brooms can be purchased for a few shillings, but while they will do many forms of sweeping admirably, they are not nearly so good as a besom for getting the leaves off the lawn or doing up a sanded path.

26 Hundreds of Things a Boy Can Make

A broom of this kind can be easily made, and will give good service for years.

Get, first of all, a stout stick about four feet long, and then collect a large bunch of twigs. Some twigs will answer better than others, those

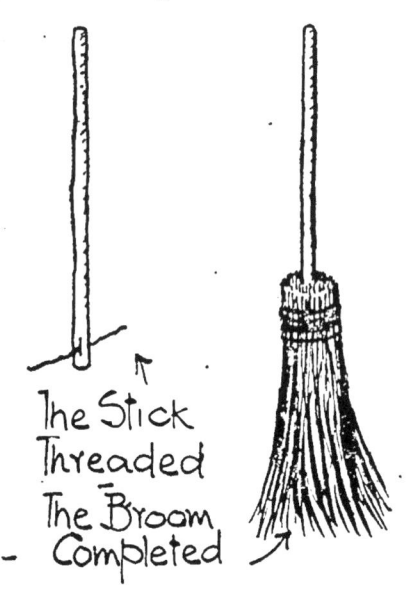

The Stick
Threaded
The Broom
- Completed

of the birch being among the best. Springy ones which do not lose their elasticity are needed.

Close to the lower end of the stick, bore a hole, and then thread a piece of galvanized wire through it. Now arrange the twigs around the stick, and when you have put an equal amount all round, take the wire thread and tie it round and round the twigs. If necessary, clip away any pieces of the twigs which spoil the symmetry of the broom.

AN AERIAL ROPEWAY

This increasingly popular form of transporting goods suggests an up-to-date mechanical toy which will provide a great deal of amusement.

The first necessity is a pair of stout wooden uprights, suitably weighted so that they will not pull over. Wood one inch square in section and about six inches high will be suitable, if each upright is firmly screwed to a square wooden base, having sides three inches long.

Near the top of each post fix a pulley wheel, the two being at the same height up the posts.

Now stand one post on a table and the other on an adjoining sideboard, the idea being that there should be a deep gap between them

Next run an endless strip of stout, flexible wire from one pulley wheel to the other and see that it is quite tight.

The ropeway is finished; but a truck is wanted to complete the equipment. Diagram A shows a suitable pattern. The body can be made of cardboard or sheet iron and the hooks and slinging frame of stout zinc wire.

To work the model, place the truck on the endless wire at B and rotate the pulley at C. When the truck reaches C it is unloaded, and on twisting the pulley at B it is brought back to the starting-point.

Another way to set up the ropeway is to attach a fixed single wire to the posts, to hang the truck to the wire by means of two of the contrivances shown at D, and to haul it backwards and forwards with thin string. The contrivance D is a curtain roller, such as can be bought for a halfpenny.

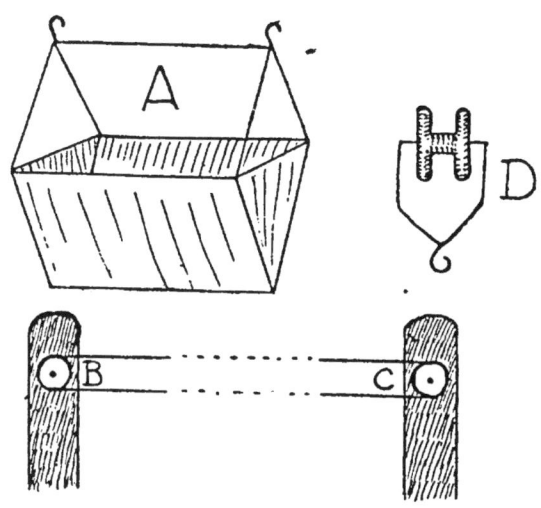

A MODEL AEROPLANE

Model aeroplanes are always fascinating, and if they really fly, so much the better. In the accompanying sketch we give a very attractive design for one. It can be made of a variety of materials, but the lighter they are the better. One thing is certain, and that is that any model which is actually flown will soon become damaged. It is, therefore, not wise to lavish too much care on the paint and ornamental work, unless the model is to be preserved as a museum specimen.

Do not make the model too small, since the details in small ones are most difficult to manage. We suggest, as a minimum, an 8 inch wing span, and a similar length from propeller to rudder. Between the wings let there be a height of 2 inches, and the propeller 2 inches from tip to tip.

For the wings use one of the following :—

(a) Thin tough white card.
(b) Sheet aluminium.
(c) Thin card for the lower deck, and a light wooden frame for the upper deck. Cover the frame with oiled silk or grease-proof paper.

The struts between the two decks should be arranged first vertically, and then diagonally. Wood laths, the thickness of a match, make admirable vertical struts, but thin wire is best for bracing the diagonals. Bind the angle joins in every case with silk thread.

The fuselage should be a skeleton of wood, covered with tough paper. It is a good idea to leave the under side open, or to tuck in the paper covering. This allows us to inspect the winder whenever necessary.

Make the two ends of the fuselage of light wood, and fix at either end a small hooked screw, as shown in the illustration. Slip an elastic band on to these and twist the propeller round. The elastic becomes knotted,

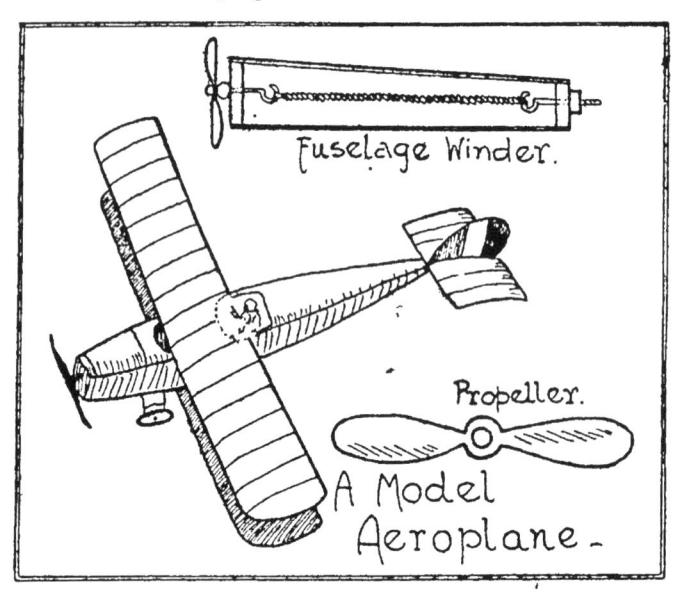

and when released drives the propeller round at a considerable rate, causing the model to fly.

Shape the propeller out of thin tin, and twist the blades so that they cut the wind. All other details of construction may be gathered from the diagrams.

A WINDER FOR MODEL AEROPLANES

Aeroplanes that are propelled by means of a twisted band of rubber

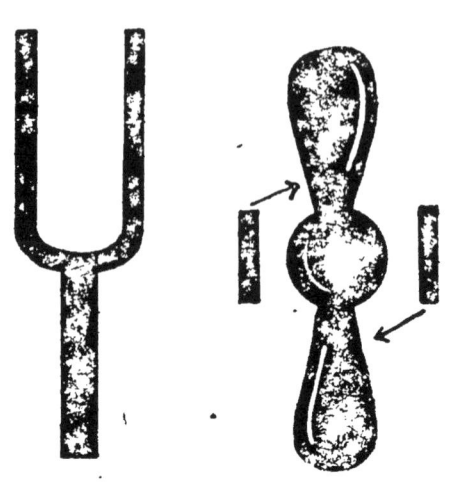

are somewhat tedious to fly because the twisting takes up so much time. Here is an extremely cute way of considerably shortening this operation.

Make the fork-shaped contrivance shown in the illustration, using 16SWG brass, a quarter of an inch thick, for the prongs, and a piece of quarter-inch round rod for the handle.

When required for use slip the handle in the chuck of a geared brace and tighten it up exactly as though it were an ordinary "bit." Put the tips of the two prongs, one on either side of the propeller, as shown in the right-hand sketch, get someone to hold the plane, and then revolve the handle of the brace. As it is geared, a comparatively few turns will knot up the rubber to its full pitch.

A KITE FOR WINDY WEATHER

If you have a large open space close to where you live, such as a meadow or a common, a kite will help you to pass many pleasant hours. It is quite an easy thing to make, and most of the materials will be found in the home so the cost will be practically nothing

First get two laths of wood, 4 feet and 3 feet long. They should be light in substance, say 1 inch broad and ⅜ inch thick. Spruce is the best wood to have, but anything will do if this special kind is not available.

When you have the laths, take the smaller length and find the centre or half-way position. Now get an old tin, such as an empty condensed milk tin, pull it to pieces, and cut out of it a flat sheet 3 or 4 inches square. Fix this sheet, diamond-wise, exactly on the centre of the lath by means of at least four small nails, evenly spaced out. Next, measure off 1½ feet from an end of the longer lath, and at the point found fix the diamond-shaped tin with four more nails. The idea of using the diamond of tin is to give rigidity to the cross we have now made. Extra strength can be produced by fixing thin laths which join up the four tips of the cross.

The wood being shaped, you must beg some calico or gay coloured cretonne from your mother, and fix it so as to cover the cross and the spaces between the limbs. The material may sag or flap about in the wind, so before fixing it to the cross, it is well to bind the edges with a piece of cord. This done, we put a screw eye in the upright arm of the cross, 4 or 5 inches from the top, to hold the string, and down at the bottom we add a long tail. This is made by screwing up lengths of coloured paper and twisting string round them every two or three inches.

Your kite should now fly, but if it does not, do not be disappointed. Just experiment with different lengths of tail until you get it right. One day the wind will suit a long tail; another, a shorter length will be best.

If you use plain calico, paint some distinctive device on it, and make it look out of the common.

A FLYING HELICOPTER

Perhaps you do not know what a flying helicopter is like. It is a winged device which, when spun, soars high into the air. Great fun can be derived by seeing to what heights it will rise. You can make one fairly easily and it will provide you with hours of enjoyment.

Get a circle of very thin tinned iron. Just the thing for the purpose is the airtight cap which is cut out of a tin of fifty Gold Flake cigarettes. Having procured the metal sheet, cut it into a circle, and pencil the outline of three propeller blades, then shape them with scissors, as shown in diagram A. Now, take some stout wire that will not easily bend force it into a circle, slightly smaller than the original circle of tinned iron, and solder the ends. The next thing is to place the propeller blades centrally on the ring of wire, turn the projecting ends over the wire, and solder them neatly. This done, make cuts in the blades, then bend them at an angle and pierce the centre with three holes. Diagram B shows exactly what you must aim at.

Three more little articles must now be contrived. For the first, take an empty cotton spool, and put in it two pegs at such a distance apart that they will fit into the two outer holes in the propeller blades. These

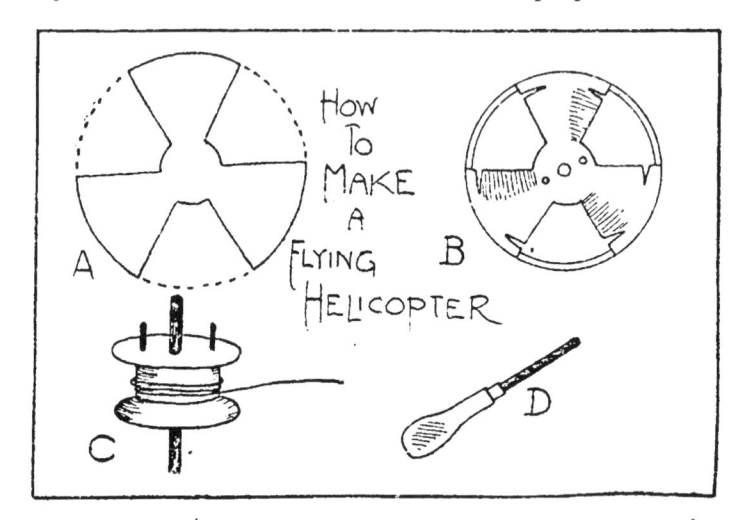

pegs can be made easily by cutting inch lengths from the stout part of two large French nails. (Diagram C.) The second article is a holder. For this procure the wooden handle of an old screw-driver, and, instead of the ordinary piece of metal, insert a rod of iron, six to eight inches long. See that it holds firmly in the handle, and is of a suitable gauge for running through the centre hole of the propeller blades. (Diagram D.) The last requirement is a length of cord.

Now for the way this little contrivance works. Hold the handle of the screwdriver in the left hand, drop the spool on to the rod, and place the helicopter on to the top of it. Now wind the string tightly round the reel and then pull firmly. The metal wheel will rise off its seating rod and soar up into the air. By winding the cord just tight enough, and pulling with sufficient strength, the blades will rise to a great height. Note that the contrivance should not be held quite vertical, but tilted slightly away from your person, in order that it may not dash against you. See also that nobody is standing in front of you! Keep your onlookers at your side, or well in the rear. Only use the apparatus in a big open space.

ANOTHER HELICOPTER

Have you an Archimedean drill? Should you possess one that has seen better days and will no longer do its ordinary job, here is a capital toy you can make of it.

First unscrew any brass caps or collars that may be fitted to its drilling tip, and leave nothing but the twisted column, the travelling bobbin, and the handle. Now cut a piece of tin into the shape of two connected propeller blades and slightly bend each blade sideways. Deflect one to the left, the other to the right. Next bore a round hole in the centre, where the two blades meet, and see that its diameter is very slightly larger than the diameter of the column of the drill.

To use, hold the drill upright, slip the propeller on to the twisted column, and let it twirl itself down to the travelling bobbin. Then, with a smart jerk, run the bobbin up the column. The propeller is pushed up before it and flies high into the air.

It is advisable to make several of these propellers as they travel so far that they are easily lost.

MAKING A BIRD TABLE

Many boys take a great interest in birds, and their especial delight is to see that those which visit their gardens in winter are properly fed. To throw food on the ground for them is a kindly act ; nevertheless, it often proves to be dangerous, as cats get to know where birds are likely to congregate. Pussy secretes himself behind some obstacle and, when a number of our feathered friends are eating the crumbs we have provided, pounces upon them, with disastrous consequences.

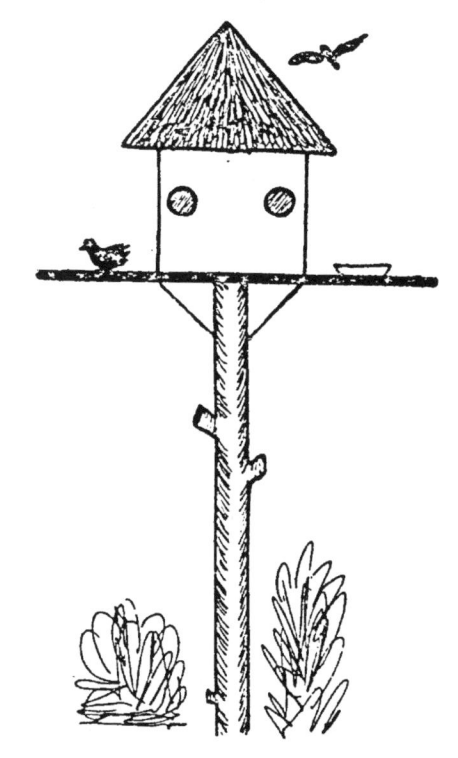

A bird table, however, makes bird feeding absolutely safe. The table consists of a flat piece of wood about a foot square, screwed to the top of a 6 foot pole. The screws are reinforced by a couple of brackets fixed to the pole and to the underside of the flat top. The foot of the pole is driven into the ground, the position chosen being such that no cat can jump off a low roof, a wall or an overhanging branch on to the table.

Suitable food for the table consists of crumbs, pieces of fat, and many kinds of cereals, but cocoa-nut is considered harmful. Do not forget a saucerful of warm water in frosty weather.

BLOWING UP YOUR FOOTBALL

More footballs are spoiled by being badly blown up than by hard wear. There is a right and a wrong way of blowing them up, and, strange to say, a good many boys do it the wrong way. Messrs. Thomlinson, Ltd., of Glasgow, who make the " Greban " football, are experts in the matter of inflating and lacing footballs. First, they suggest that the unfilled ball should have the tongue drawn out ; then the bladder is rolled up loosely and inserted into the case, the tube being passed through the tongue. When this is done, the ball is shaken lightly, in order that the rolled bladder may be unwound.

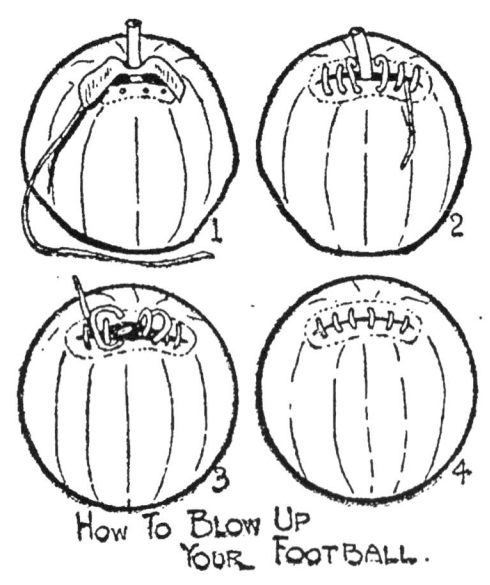

How To Blow Up Your Football.

Second, the tongue is slipped into position and the mouth is laced completely. Notice particularly that the two end laps of the lace must be drawn tight, and that the two centre laps of the lace must be left loosely looped, as shown, so as to allow the tube to be inserted after inflation.

Third, the ball is fully inflated and the tube tied securely. Then use any handy blunt instrument to raise the mouth facing sufficient to allow for the tucking-in of the tube. It is possible to push the tube under either side of the opening, but it is correct to insert it below the facing opposite that to which the tongue is stitched. Never tuck it under the stitched side.

Fourth, it will now be found that all lace loops can be drawn taut

Hundreds of Things a Boy Can Make

without any undue strain, either on the lace or the lace holes. Pass the ends of the lace below the laps, as shown, and the result will be a smooth and well-closed mouth.

Next time you blow up your football, follow these instructions, and see if you do not agree that they are sound. Since adopting them, we have never had to stop the play in order that a projecting lace-end, or the tip of the tube, may be returned to its proper place.

A BALL FOR WINDY WEATHER

This little paper ball will refuse to keep still if let loose on a windy day, as long as it can roll and tumble and scurry forward on a smooth surface, such as is provided by your school playground or the dry sand on the beach at the seaside. It will give you endless fun, especially if you and your friend make one each and have races.

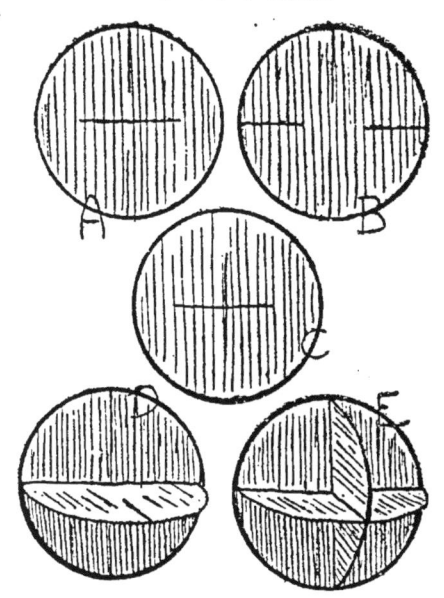

Cut three circles as shown in A, B and C. Fit A into B (see D) and then complete the finished ball, E, by tucking in C. Make each circle an inch and a half in diameter and use stout drawing paper. It is not a bad idea to colour the circles and sides with different bright paints.

IS IT GOING TO RAIN?

Everybody knows the pictorial barometers which foretell the weather by means of slips of paper that change colour. What is not so well known is how the sensitive paper is made. Here is the way:

Make up the following solution:

(1) Cobalt chloride, ½ ounce.
(2) Sodium chloride, ¼ ounce.
(3) Calcium chloride, 40 grains.
(4) Gum arabic, ½ ounce.
(5) Water, 2 to 2½ ounces.

Though none of these chemicals are costly, it will probably be cheaper to have the formula made up at a chemist, than to buy quantities of each of the ingredients.

When the solution has been well shaken, to see that all the crystals have been dissolved, pour a small quantity into a clean photographic dish and immerse pieces of unused white blotting paper. Allow each piece to remain floating for five minutes, then hang up to dry by pinning one corner. When dry, cut the paper into fancy shapes and use for decorative purposes. One suggestion is to draw a girl on the back of a postcard, and to use a shaped piece of the paper for her dress. Do not stick the paper down by pasting all over the reverse side; either paste along a narrow edge at the top, or cut slits in the card and fold ears of the paper through them.

The paper serves as a barometer, because, when it is bluish, the weather will be fine and dry; but if changeable wet weather is approaching, the paper turns a lilac-pinkish colour. If decidedly pink, it heralds very wet and stormy weather.

A BOY'S BAROMETER

You can easily make a very reliable barometer if you are able to procure a large glass jam-jar and a globular bottle with a fairly long, straight neck—an empty Chianti bottle is admirable for the purpose.

A barometer, as you know, tells if we are going to have fine or wet weather, and its action depends on the weight of the air. To make your barometer, place the bottle upside down in the jam-jar, so that the bulging sides rest on the collar of the jar, and the neck of the bottle is at

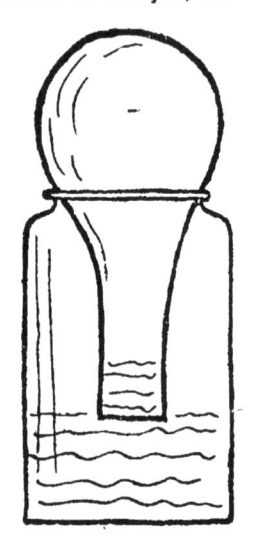

least three inches from the bottom of the jar. Inside the jar there must be some water. Just how much does not exactly matter, but it is well to arrange it so that on a wet, stormy day it just reaches the neck of the bottle. It is wise, in fact, to wait for such a day on which to make the barometer. When the weather improves, the water will rise slightly up the inverted bottle neck.

The readings of your barometer will be as follows :—
1. No water in the neck—stormy and wet.
2. A little water in the neck—change.
3. More water in the neck—fine and dry.
4. Water tending to rise in the neck—weather improving.
5. Water tending to fall in the neck—weather becoming unsettled.

A TOP THAT SPINS IN THE AIR

This is a very wonderful top because, unlike the ordinary ones, it will spin in the air. First procure a post card and cut out of it a circle two and a half inches in diameter. Be very careful that you do not buckle the card, because, if you do, it will catch the wind at the wrong angle when it is spun, and fall to the ground.

Next draw about six rectangles on the circle in the positions shown in Diagram A. Note that they do not follow each other round the circle in a ring ; but each is set at an angle which you must imitate fairly closely. Then, with a sharp pocket-knife, cut along all the edges of each

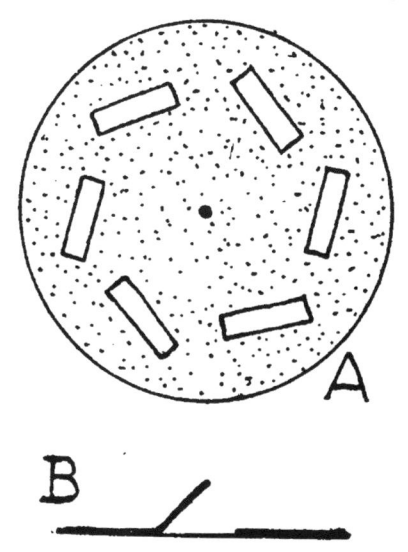

rectangle, except the one nearest to the circumference, and bend up the rectangles so that they form little flaps. The second diagram shows how much they should be bent.

When this is done, push a pin through the centre of the circle in such a way that the pin-head is underneath and so that no more than three-quarters of the body of the pin appears above.

It must be pushed through absolutely vertically, so to keep it upright, cut a little circle of stamp paper, lick it, and push it over the pin-point and stick it on to the card.

Now take something that you can blow through, such as a pea-shooter, a cigarette holder, or any piece of piping. Hold the tube—whatever it is—upright and put the toy-top just under the lower end, keeping it there with the finger-tip. As you blow down the tube, the top begins to revolve and, in a second, you can take away your finger ; but the top will go on spinning gaily. It will continue to do so as long as you have breath to blow.

If you cannot get the top to go properly, it is probably because the pin is not quite vertical, the circle is bent or the card is too thick and heavy.

SIX MAGIC TOPS

When you have an evening to spare and cannot go out to play in the open, here is a capital way of passing an interesting hour or so. Procure some pieces of cardboard—unstamped post cards will serve admirably—and cut out half a dozen circular discs, about 3 inches in diameter. Take two or three wooden meat skewers, cheap pen-holders, or other pieces of wood of similar shape, and cut them into 3 inch lengths, sharpening one end of each to a rather blunt point. Push one of these pieces through the centre of each disc, so that $\frac{3}{4}$ inch remains above the disc and $2\frac{1}{4}$ inches stand below. You now have a number of tops which can easily be spun by twirling the upper part of the peg between the thumb and index finger.

Before you fit the wooden peg paint the discs as follows :—

1. Divide one disc into seven equal parts, and paint them in this order : red, orange, yellow, green, blue, indigo, and violet. When the top is spun rapidly the colours will disappear, and the resulting effect will be a dull grey.

2. Draw an eight-rayed star on another disc and paint it, say, red. When spun the disc will appear red in the centre, and then the colour will gradually fade away until the edge of the circle will be white.

3. Again draw an eight-rayed star, but this time leave the star white and paint the remaining parts red. In this case the disc, when spun, will be white in the centre and dark red at the circumference.

4. On the fourth disc draw a diameter, and colour one half blue and the other yellow. The disc, when revolved quickly, will show up green.

5. Draw about eight radii on the fifth disc and put short cross lines on the radii. The spinning disc will appear to be ornamented with a number of concentric rings.

6. We leave this disc for a design of your own planning. What curious pattern can you suggest ?

A TOY LAWN ROLLER

Small children take a keen delight in playing with miniature copies of the things with which their parents work. Take for instance, a lawn roller. Whilst father is none too pleased at having to drag the heavy roller backwards and forwards across the lawn, his small child would be only too delighted to have a toy roller, so that he could do his bit.

The obvious thing is to make a miniature roller and let the young hopeful follow his desires. First, hunt out a fairly large cylindrical tin possessing a well-fitting lid. In the centre of the lid, and, also, in the bottom, punch a small hole and pass a piece of stout wire through ; then run a streak of solder round the rim of the lid and fix it on permanently.

Now bend the wire carefully and symmetrically, so that the two ends join up above the mid-point of one of the sides, and there fix it to a T piece of wood. Let the vertical stroke of the T be about two feet long.

Smooth the wood and coat the tin with a lead-coloured paint, the wire green, and the wood a bright red.

This toy will give pleasure to a small child every time his father attends to the lawn.

CRYSTAL BELLS

The following is an idea which came from Japan. Make a ring of metal or cardboard, as shown in the diagram. Let it be three-quarters of an inch wide and from four to six inches in diameter. While the strip is still flat punch about a dozen holes in it, equidistant; then form the ring and join the ends by means of solder or by lacing them with wire or cotton. Glue will do when cardboard is used.

Next obtain some thin string, preferably coloured, and a number of small pieces of glass. As the size of the pieces matters very little, it will be possible to shape them with a cheap cutter. If tinted glass of various hues cannot be had, use clear glass and colour it with paint, or stick pieces of coloured tissue paper to it.

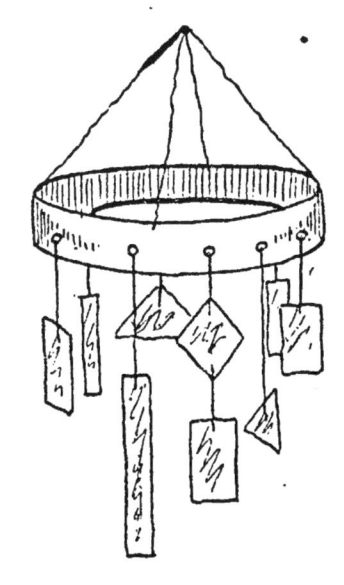

Now use the string of various lengths for supporting the little pieces of glass. A small square of stamp paper will hold the string to the glass; but do not suspend it until the paper has dried.

Hang this attractive toy in a doorway and every movement of the air will make the glasses tinkle pleasantly.

WATER FROM NOWHERE

Have you seen, in shop windows, a teapot pouring out tea, for hours on end without being replenished? To add to the mystery, the pot is suspended by a fine cord, showing plainly that the supply cannot come through the source which appears to be the most likely one.

This idea of providing unlimited quantities of liquid which apparently come from nowhere can be utilised to mystify your friends in the following way.

Obtain two pieces of glass tubing of different diameter. One must be able to slip within the other, and have a certain amount of space to spare. Make a right-angled bend in both of them. Let the bend be a foot from one end of the narrower tube and three or four inches from the end of the other. The length of the remaining arms is immaterial, but about four inches will be suitable. When you have done this, seal up the end of the four-inch arm of the stouter tube. The diagram shows these pieces exactly as they are required.

Now, let us think of the way they have to be fitted up. Suppose you have a pond in the garden, with a fountain in the middle. Slip a piece of rubber tubing to the supply pipe and bring it up close to the surface of the water; then fit on the tube with the narrower gauge, so that the arm, measuring about a foot, points upwards.

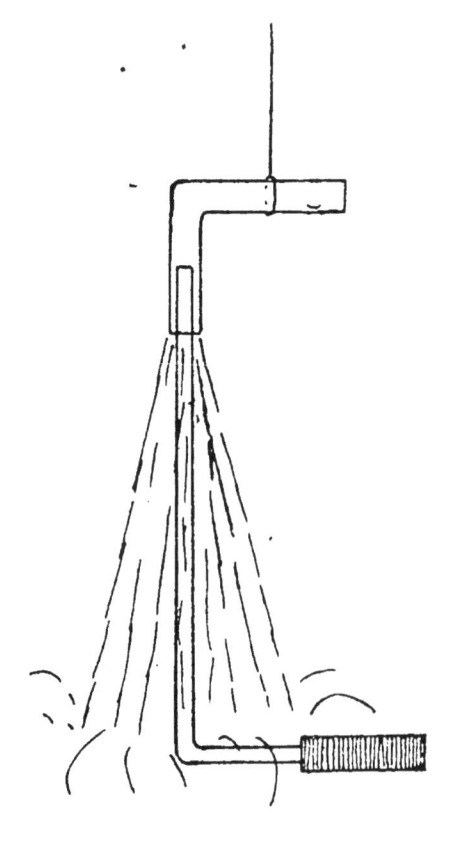

Next, take the wider-gauge tube; put it vertically over the first tube and let the narrower piece enter the wider piece to the extent of about an inch and a half. Support the upper piece, in this position, by means of a cord, suspended to a post, an overhanging tree, or anything available.

Now, turn on the water gently. It will run up the lower glass tube, into the upper one and, finding no other way out, it will pour down the sides of the lower tube, which it will completely hide. It will appear

Hundreds of Things a Boy Can Make 39

as though the upper tube contains unlimited quantities of water, yet it is obviously a short piece of piping which cannot hold a great deal. That is where the mystery comes in.

If you have no pond in your garden, the illusion may be performed in the bath or in the scullery sink, but it is more difficult then to obscure the lower part of the arrangement.

THE JOLLY ANGLERS

Fishing is forbidden by law during certain seasons of the year; but the fishing which we suggest here is unaffected by such restrictions.

Get about a dozen corks, steady each with a stout nail driven in at the bottom face, and force into the upper face of each a small piece of tin cut to look like the head of a fish. Coming out of all the fishes' mouths

must be a little hook. Pieces of tin suitable for the purpose can be found in almost any home. The circular lid cut out of a tin containing condensed milk, for instance, will answer quite well. Do the cutting with scissors, if shears or snips are not available, but it is not advisable to use the best pair in the house.

Each jolly angler who takes part in the game should have a stick, provided with a length of cotton, to which is attached a bent pin.

Sit on chairs, placed the same distance from the water, and let the winner be the player who catches most fish in a quarter of an hour.

POLES FOR NET-BALL

Although boys do not play net-ball to any great extent, it is certainly their privilege to make the necessary poles, so that their sisters may indulge in the game.

Two poles comprise a set. Each is fitted, at the top, with a metal hoop, to which is attached a hanging net. At the bottom of the pole is a foot to enable it to stand erect.

For each pole, you will require ten feet of wood, two and a quarter inches square in section. Smooth the sides well with glass paper to remove all splinters. For the metal hoop, take some fairly stout galvanized iron wire and lace three or four strands together. Then bend it into a circle, pass the free ends through a hole made in the post and

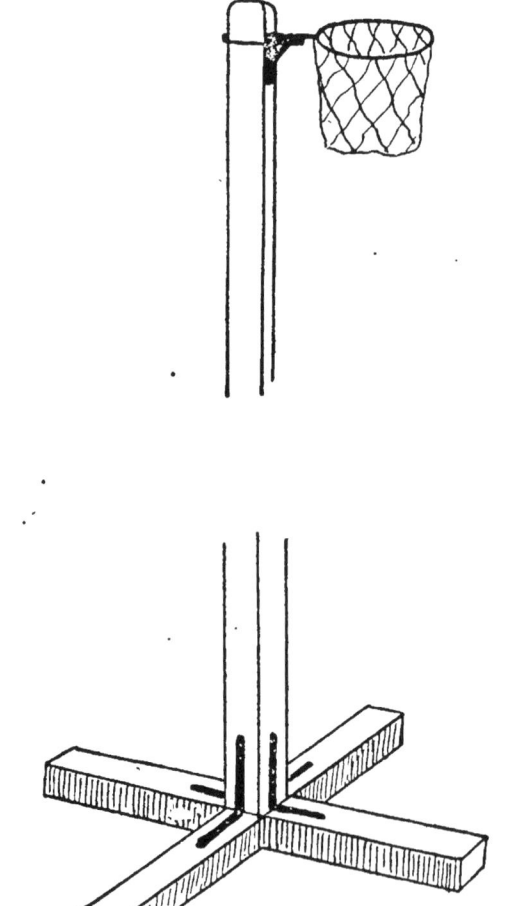

bind it round the wood. The circle should stand at least three inches away from the post, and at this point, the laced wire should be supported by an iron L piece.

The lower end of the post is screwed to a flat cross of wood, each limb of which should be a foot long. For additional strength an L piece must be screwed to the four faces of the pole and, also, to the four portions of the cross.

The net, itself, is hardly a boy's job and you had better leave it to your sister. She will make a loose meshed net of string, the lower opening being slightly larger than that of the upper opening. The hoop should be large enough to permit the passing of an ordinary football with a trifle to spare.

THE BIRD IN THE HAND

This attractive toy makes a realistic bird-like whizzing noise when the wooden handle is held and the arm is swung round so that the bird flies in a circle or follows the course of a figure eight. The more quickly it is revolved the higher and shriller becomes the note.

To make this musical toy, first obtain a three-inch length of fairly stout wire. To one end glue two pieces of very thin wood, marked A in the diagram. Strips of wood taken from the edges of an empty match-box will do for this part of the construction.

Next cut an inch off the end of a round pencil, bore out the lead, and slip this wooden tube over the wire. It must be able to move up and down the wire quite freely. Then twist up the free end of the wire and make a knot to prevent the tube flying off. (See B, marked on the diagram.)

Now draw two birds on a sheet of paper, in such a way that when cut out and pasted round the short length of pencil they will exactly overlap each other. When pasting the two together imprison the tip of a length of thread between them, and carry the other end of the thread to the head of a short stick. The total length of the thread should be about fifteen inches.

When the paste has dried hard, whizz the stick round in a circle and the musical note will be sounded.

THE BOOMERANG THAT IS DIFFERENT

Here is an unusual type of boomerang. Cut out the cross, shown in the diagram, and let it be about two inches long. Make it of thin card that is about the same substance as a visiting card.

To use it squeeze one of the limbs between the flesh and the nail of your left-hand thumb and keep it horizontally. Then, tap smartly on

one of the side limbs with your right-hand index finger. Away sails the cross, but presently, it curves round and comes back towards you.

A HOME-MADE AQUARIUM

A well-kept aquarium is a most interesting possession, but very few aquaria are properly cared for. If you have an idea that you would like to keep a few goldfish, do not buy the usual bell-jar aquarium. It is easily knocked over and broken, and it is a most uncomfortable home for its inmates. A far better contrivance is readily made if you can handle a soldering iron with success. First select a stout wooden box with dimensions approximating 24 inches by 12 inches by 12 inches. One with dovetailed sides reinforced by a few long cut nails will prove admirable. The next thing is to remove one of the sides, and then to screw the bottom of the box on to a thick wooden base which projects all round the bottom. This serves to support the box, which will become heavy when full of water, and to give a grip for lifting the aquarium. After this a wooden groove or frame is fitted round the three edges of the space left by taking away the wooden side. This done, all the inner surfaces of the box are covered with thin sheet zinc, the joins being carefully soldered and rendered water tight. Even the frame to the open side must be covered with the zinc. We now go to the glazier's and buy a sheet of 32 oz. glass—plate glass is even better—to fit the open side. Put this inside the frame arrangement so that it touches everywhere. First, however, coat the frame with the mixture given below and press into good contact. It will take a fortnight to dry, but at the end of this time will be absolutely watertight.

Mix 2 oz. of fine sifted sand with 2 oz. of plaster of paris, add an equal amount of litharge, and 1 oz. of crushed resin. Stir into a stiff paste by slowly adding linseed oil and not more than one spoonful of driers All these ingredients may be purchased for a few pence at an oil-shop.

When the glass face has had time to set hard, fill the aquarium with frequent changes of water for a week. It is then ready for use.

The trouble with most aquaria is that they contain a number of fish which use up oxygen, and no steps are taken to provide a constant supply of this necessity. The consequence is the fish become sickly and die. The proper way is to aim at a correct balance, as it is called, and

Hundreds of Things a Boy Can Make 43

this can be supplied by vegetation which gives off oxygen. If this be done, there will be no need to change the water frequently, and yet the fish will live and be healthy.

To make a healthy home of your aquarium, cover the bottom with an

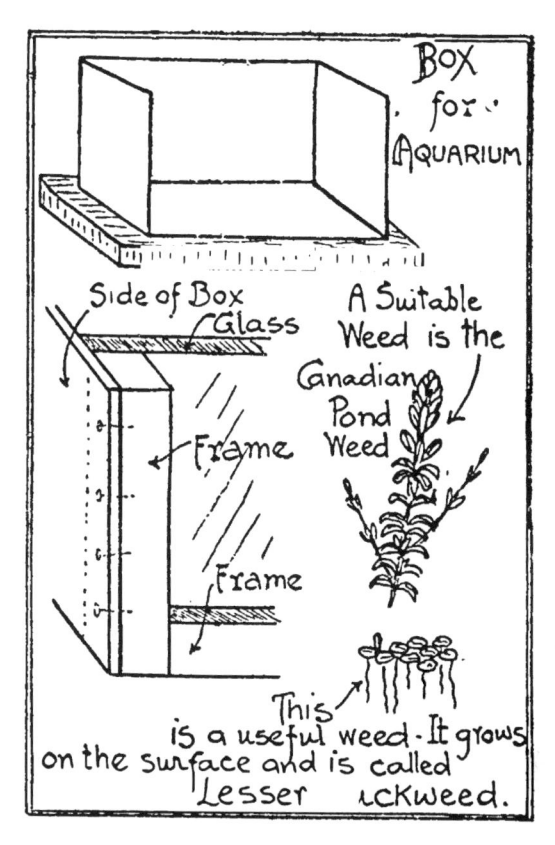

```
           BOX
           for
         AQUARIUM

    Side of Box     A Suitable
       Glass        Weed is the
                    Canadian
          Frame     Pond
                    Weed
          Frame

                This
        is a useful weed. It grows
   on the surface and is called
          Lesser  ickweed.
```

inch of well-washed sand, and in it plant half a dozen water weeds, such as may be taken from ponds. Feed the fish occasionally with small worms, but do not leave uneaten portions to decay in the water. Cover the water when dust is about, and do not stand the aquarium where the sun can cause an alternate rise and fall of the temperature of the water.

RE-ENAMELLING YOUR CYCLE

No boy can be proud of a shabby cycle and, if your machine is beginning to look the worse for wear, you should see what can be done to it.

If the enamel is not chipped or scratched but merely looks dull, the appearance may be improved considerably by putting a soft flannel in hot water, wringing it out and sponging over the tubes. Do not use a great deal of water and avoid making the frame very wet. All you want to do is to clear away the dirt and this can be done with a flannel that is merely damp. When all the surfaces have been sponged over, rub them dry with a soft cloth that cannot scratch. At this stage, it is advisable to leave the work for a day, then to go over all the parts with furniture cream and polish them. When finished, you will probably be surprised to find how fine the frame looks.

But the enamel on your cycle may be too far gone to benefit by this treatment. The best thing, then, will be to re-paint it. Naturally, you will not be able to do the work as well as it is done at the factory, because there it is stoved, and this is an operation that you cannot undertake. Nevertheless, your results ought to be almost as good, if you take pains and follow the directions given below.

You must decide whether you will take the cycle to pieces before applying the paint. Of course, the work can be done better when the frame has been dismantled, but it is not advisable to do so unless you are quite sure that you know how to re-assemble all the parts accurately.

Before applying the fresh enamel, it is very important to see that the old surfaces are in a proper condition to receive the new coats. More likely than not, scratches will be present and some of the paint will have perished. It will flake off, then, when scraped with a finger nail. Obviously, it will be wrong to paint over enamel that is in this condition. Accordingly, your best plan will be to rub over all the tubes, paying particular attention to the joints, with a medium grade of glass-paper. There is no need to rub down to the metal, if the paint is sound. All you should attempt is to smooth out scratch marks, get rid of paint that has perished and provide a bright surface, wherever there are signs of rust. This rubbing will cause a good deal of gritty dust, so it is advisable to wrap cloths round the hubs, bearings and other working parts to protect them.

When the surfaces have been nicely smoothed, obtain a tin of good, hard drying, black enamel. Pay a fair price for it and do not be tempted to save a few pence by buying a tin of cheap Japan black. Also, get a brush with soft hairs, not too large.

Now, put on the first coat. Apply the enamel sparingly and evenly and do not attempt to obliterate all the marks underneath.

If you have not been too lavish and, if the prepared surface was free from grease, the coat should dry in a few hours, then you will be able to proceed with the next stage of the work, which consists in going lightly over all the enamel with glass-paper of a fine grade. Rub down any small lumps that may be present and, in addition, remove all the shine of the paint, but do no more.

Now, put on a second coat in exactly the same way as the first. When it is dry, you must decide whether you will leave the frame as it is or provide a third coat. Two coats will, generally, look well enough at the outset, but they will not wear nearly so satisfactorily as three; accordingly we advise you to put on the third coat if you have no good reason for stopping at the second.

Of course, the rubbing-down process must be repeated, prior to the application of the third coat.

It may be that yours is an all-weather cycle or that you desire to turn your mount into one. This will mean that the hubs, handle bar and other bright parts need to be blackened, also. Since enamels refuse to dry properly on a surface soiled with dirty oil, it is imperative that such parts as the hubs must be cleaned carefully before they are coated. The best way to do this is to rub them with petrol, which, as you know, is highly inflammable.

When painting the hubs and similar working parts, be careful to see that the enamel is not permitted to clog the oil holes or run into the bearings.

There is no doubt that if a good grade of enamel is used for the above work, the final effect will be a brilliant black. It may be, however, that you consider it is, perhaps, a little too brilliant—that the appearance might be described as "sticky." If these are your views and you would prefer a more mellow surface, proceed as follows, when the final coat has been dry for at least two days:

(a) Sprinkle some pumice powder on a very damp rag and rub it lightly over the frame. Vigorous action is not wanted; stop when the surface shine has been removed.

(b) Wipe the frame with a clean damp rag, to remove the adhering particles of grit, and dry with a towel.

(c) Sprinkle some rotten-stone on a rag, moistened with olive oil, and rub very lightly, then polish with a piece of velvet cloth.

Note that lining transfers can be bought for providing the lines which are seen on some frames. They are easy to apply and cost about a shilling for a complete set.

MOTOR CAR NUMBER PLATES

If you can print, there is no reason why you should not try your hand at making a number plate for your father's car, should one be required.

Procure, first of all, a piece of stout sheet zinc or tinned iron. The regulations require that the plate should measure four and a half inches high by a little more than three times as many inches as there are letters and figures, where long shaped plates are concerned, or nine inches high by a little more than three times as many inches as there are figures in cases where the plate is of the broad shape. Therefore, let your sheet be a quarter of an inch longer each way, so that you can turn over an eighth of an inch edging all round.

Next, solder on to the back of the plate the requisite fastenings, and then give the front two coats of black cycle enamel. Put on the coats thinly so that they will dry quickly. Then, print the index letter or letters and the number in quick drying white enamel. In doing this, note that every letter and figure must be 3½ inches high and the strokes five-eighths of an inch wide; also that there must be a space of half an inch between each symbol, and that between the edges of the plate and the nearest part of the symbols there must be a space of half an inch.

YOUR MOTOR HORN

To use paint other than black, to put the index marks in any form but one or two straight lines, or to place a hyphen between the letters and number, renders you liable to a possible prosecution.

YOUR MOTOR HORN

Have you a rubber ball that has been ill-treated and has, consequently, burst? Also, have you a penny trumpet that has seen better days? If so, with the two damaged playthings you can make a really jolly motor horn.

Take the trumpet, remove the mouthpiece, if it has not already come asunder, and force the narrow end into the ball, through the hole. Of course, if the ball is slit and the slit is large it will not do.

When the trumpet is wedged tightly into the ball, squeeze the latter, and all you will now need is a Rolls-Royce to become a full-fledged motorist.

A WOODEN TIP WAGGON

A great number of youngsters derive a good deal of pleasure out of such toys as wooden lorries. Even though you may be a little too old to play with this useful vehicle, you may have a younger brother or sister who would appreciate it considerably. They will find it awfully useful for loading up and unloading with all sorts of objects, and, for them, it would be an admirable Christmas or birthday present.

The diagrams will give you some idea of the finished article, and the dimensions suggested will help you to construct it with accuracy, but let us point out that these measurements need not be followed implicitly. For instance, you may wish to use an old cigar box for the tilting compartment. All your dimensions, then, should be altered to suit the scale set by the cigar box. Certain it is that if you can improvise some handy box for this compartment, it will save a good deal of the constructional part. Also, you may have a set of wheels by you. Rather than spend money on fresh ones, it will be wise to vary the dimensions of the axles.

But to return to the diagrams. First, cut out the floor board, nine inches long by four inches wide. Any wood from three-eighths to three-quarters of an inch thick will serve. Note that the floor board has two cut out parts to fit the bonnet, which it is advisable to make three inches wide.

Hundreds of Things a Boy Can Make

The axle length for the rear wheels should be about one inch square, in section, and four and a half inches long. This will allow the wheels to clear the body of the vehicle nicely. A wheel having a diameter of from 2 to 2¾ inches will do for the back. Use the same kind of wood for the front axle, and cut it to the same length as the back, but place a layer of wood three inches square, and of the same thickness as the floor board, between it and the bonnet. This will enable a smaller pair of wheels, say 1½ to 1¾ inches in diameter, to be used. Fix all the wheels by means of screws. Drill the holes neatly and horizontally and there will then be no trouble with them, even if used roughly. Arrange these holes not necessarily in the centre of the axle ends, but at such heights, as when the wheels are fitted, the lorry will stand horizontally. This can only be determined by trial.

The tilting body, if a box is not used, should be made of the same wood

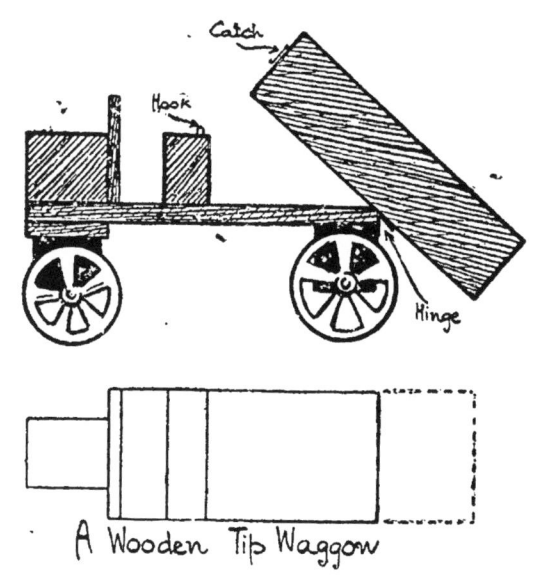

A Wooden Tip Waggon

as the floor board. It will be preferable to mortise the ends rather than pin them flush. The necessary indentations can be made easily with a fret-saw. Let the body or box be about nine inches long, and exactly the same width as the chassis.

The best way to fit the tilting body will be to put two big hinges on the back of the rear axle, and fix them to the under floor of the body. This will provide for the swinging action. To keep the body secure, put a small hook on the centre of the driver's seat, and a brass catch on the front of the body. This will fasten it down and hold it firmly when the lorry is loaded.

When the wood-work has been assembled, and before the wheels are fixed, a coat or two of paint will be necessary. Of course a varnish paint will look best, but it takes a good time to dry. If desirous of getting the job done quickly, use an oil paint which dries with a matt surface. This will be hard in an hour or more. One colour for the whole vehicle, if of a bright hue, will please quite young children, but for older youngsters, it will be well to ornament the bonnet so that it really looks like a bonnet,

48   *Hundreds of Things a Boy Can Make*

to provide the regulation number plates, and to add the name and address of the proud owner by printing it on a small slip of paper, pasted low down on the near side.

A WORKING CRANE

A working crane will afford you hours of amusement. This is how you can make one fairly easily. Cut the following parts in the wood indicated:

(1) A base 5 inches long, 4 inches wide, and 1 inch thick. A substantial piece of wood is needed to keep the crane steady.

(2) Two side supports, triangular in shape, each side 5 inches. Use wood an inch thick.

(3) A movable base 4 inches long, 3 inches wide, and half an inch thick.

(4) A crane arm 9 inches long and an inch square in section.

(5) Two axle-pieces for carrying the wheels, each 4 inches long and an inch square in section.

(6) Four wooden wheels about one and a half inches in diameter. On no account may they be as much as 2 inches.

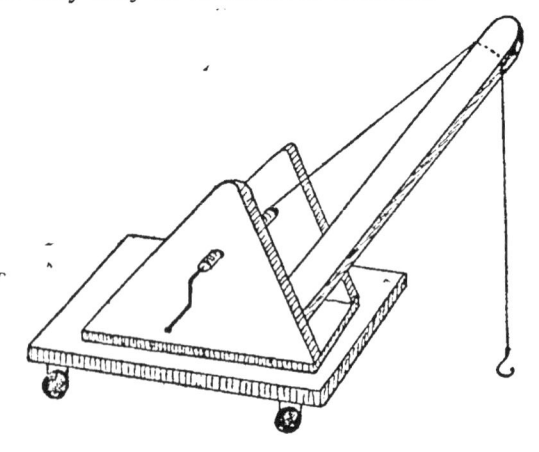

To assemble the various parts, begin with the base and glue and nail all the joins. First fix the axles half an inch from the ends of the base. Then stand the side supports upright upon the movable base and join along the bottom edges. Cut a wedge-shaped piece from one end of the crane arm, so that when it stands flat on the new surface it makes an angle of sixty degrees with the horizontal. Place it centrally on the forepart of the movable base and screw from below. In the angle of sixty degrees, formed by the arm and the movable base, fit a sloping block of wood to give the arm strength. Then near the upper part of the triangular side run a piece of stout wire, a short metal rod, or a length of dowelling, and form one end into a handle. Use stout wire for the purpose. In the upper end of the crane arm make a smooth groove about half an inch deep.

To fit the movable base to the fixed base, make a central hole through both and put in a nut and bolt. Fix the wheels with long screws, being careful to run them in straight, and see that the wheels do not rise as high as the upper edge of the fixed base. Lastly, tie tightly a piece of good, fine cord to the winding rod of dowelling (or whatever was used), run it up into the slot, cut in the crane arm, and let a good length hang over. At the loose end fix a hook.

A CRICKET SCORE BOARD

Does your cricket club possess a score board ? If not, why don't you make them one ?

The requirements are:

(1) A post, 8 feet in length and 2½ inches square, in section.
(2) A flat board, with a surface of about 3½ by 2½ feet.
(3) A cross-shaped foot, each limb of which is about 12 inches long.
(4) A set of number plates.

The construction is not difficult. When the post has been trimmed up and smoothed, the board is made. Most likely, short lengths of wood with cross strips, fixed to the back, will be used for this purpose. The board will be joined to the post by means of, at least, six long screws. The foot is constructed in the same way as the base of a net-ball post (which see).

When the various pieces have been put together, the whole is painted a dark colour, preferably black, and, then, three rows of hooks, three each top and bottom, two in centre, are screwed into the face of the board.

The uppermost row of hooks is to record the total score for the innings ; the second row, for registering the number of wickets down ; and the third row for putting up the score of the last batsman.

You will want a set of number plates. These consist of metal sheets, each about 10 by 8 inches, with a hole in the middle of the upper edge. Sheet zinc serves admirably for the purpose, so long as the edges are smoothed after being cut. Two coats of black paint should be applied, then the numbers can be painted boldly in white. Usually, each plate is inscribed with a number on both faces, and about twenty-five plates comprise a set.

MAKING A SCOOTER

Every home where there are children must have a scooter. We, of course, have one, and this is how it is made. First, let it be said, the one we made was for a child of six, and the measurements were chosen accordingly ; for taller children they must, of course, be increased.

At the outset we decided that we had not the tools to make the wheels properly, and as you will probably be in the same fix you had better buy them, as we did. Should you decide to purchase them, get them before you draw up your plans, as the scooter must be built round the wheels. Our wheels are wooden, with rubber tyres, and they cost threepence each. You need a pair. Although iron ones will last longer they are not advised, as they jolt and make a terrible noise.

We first of all made the steering head (Fig. 1). For this a strip of wood 26 inches by 2¼ inches and 1 inch thick was used. The head was shaped as shown, and the slot for the wheel was arranged to give the wheel an inch clearance. It will probably be easiest to run the drill through the wood for the axle hole before the wheel slot is cut. Use a long bolt

D

for the axle, and fix it with a washer and nut. See that it runs truly and freely.

The next thing is to make the footplate. This was a rectangular piece of wood, 20 inches by 2¼ inches and 1 inch thick. A slot for the wheel was cut and the axle hole drilled, as in the previous case (Fig. 3).

The two main portions were made in less than half an hour, and it then remained to join them by a bracket arrangement. The shop-made articles are often constructed with a wooden bracket, but we advise a metal one, as it is much stronger and more satisfactory.

We had the bracket made by a blacksmith. Fig. 2 shows its shape, and it was fashioned out of strip metal one inch wide. The bar that

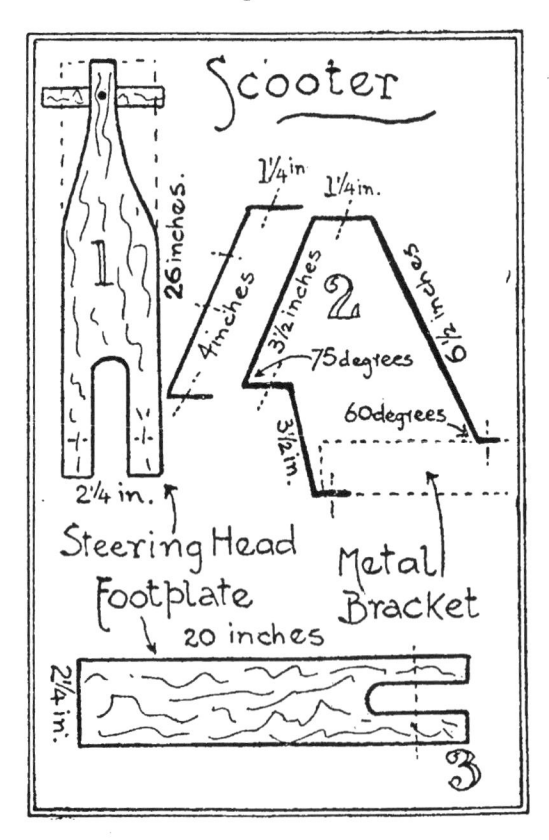

runs parallel to the steering head takes an angle at the bottom of 75 degrees, while the down run that reaches the foot plate has an angle of 60 degrees.

Draw diagram 2 full size, take it to a blacksmith, and he will make it for about one shilling. Note that two pieces are needed, as shown. Indicate where the bolt holes are to come. We have suggested their positions by cross lines.

Having obtained this bracket, bolt it to the footplate, so that the latter stands horizontally when engaged to the steering head. A long rod, with a round head at the top end and an eye hole at the bottom, sufficiently large to take a split pin, joins the two portions of the scooter.

It remains to fix a handle grip on the steering head (see Fig 1), to rub all the parts smooth, to give the wood a coat of white hard varnish, and the metal a covering of Japan black.

A KIDDIE'S SEAT SCOOTER

Small children are not big enough for ordinary scooters, yet they love to have something on which they can ride about. This duck seat scooter is the very thing for them, and being built low, there is no fear of the riders tumbling off and causing themselves harm. Moreover, this little toy is easily made, and you will be able to construct one in about three hours.

First, look well at the diagram and note the various parts. You will want at the outset a piece of wood, an inch and a half thick, about 18 inches long, and from 8 to 12 inches wide, according to the length of the legs of the kiddie for whom you are making it.

Having obtained the wood, mark on it a shape approximating that shown in the illustration, and cut it out with a saw that is springy enough to bend just sufficiently.

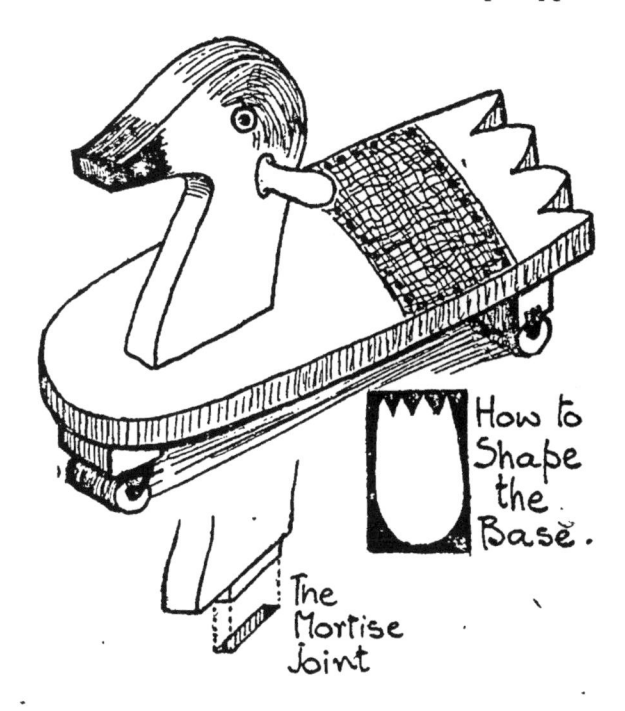

Out of wood of the same thickness, cut the head, making it from 10 to 12 inches high. You must now mortise the joint, because if nails or screws are used the head will soon come off. Mortising, though it looks hard, is not difficult if you have one or two sharp chisels.

The head being fixed, screw in two handle grips, or if you prefer it, bore right through the head and fit one long grip.

Now, take some 2 inch quartering, fix a length about 8 inches long at the back, and a square block of it at the front. On to these pieces, screw three chair casters, but be sure that they lean backwards, or they will drag and not run.

If you intend to make an extra good job of the toy, take a piece of leather or soft carpet, put some springy padding under it, and then nail it down with brass-headed nails on to the base-board, where it will serve as a nice-cushioned seat.

Lastly, paint all the wood with two coats of enamel, using white for the body, black for the beak and eyes, and green for the top of the head. The edge of the base-board will look well if done in red.

A PAIR OF STILTS

Walking on stilts is fine fun, and, moreover, it strengthens the muscles of the legs and affords good exercise. If you are thinking about making a pair, do not have them too tall. 18 inches off the ground will be quite high enough for the leg-rests, and there will be less distance to fall should you lose your balance.

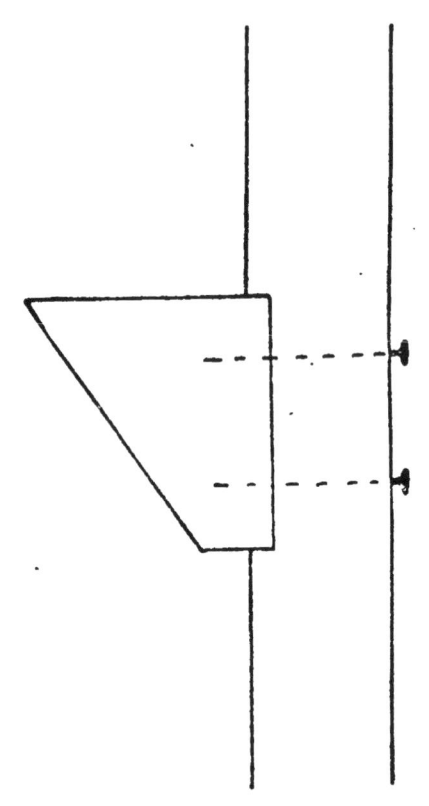

Probably the best way to construct them will be to procure two 6-foot lengths of wood that is 2 inches square in section. Be very careful to see that the pieces are perfectly sound and that the grain does not run across the lengths and so offer a good opportunity for snapping.

Fit the foot-rests as shown in the diagram. Mind they are recessed slightly, because if they are merely screwed to the side of the wood there is considerable likelihood of the screws loosening.

When the rests are fixed shave away the square edges of the poles from the top to the rests and make them circular. Do not round off the edges below the leg-rests. Then go over the whole of the surfaces with glass-paper and make them quite smooth and devoid of splinters. Round off the upper ends.

If, when using, the stilts, you find them a little too long, it is a simple matter to cut them down, but be careful that the two poles are made exactly alike.

MAKING A WALKING-STICK

The easiest way to make a walking-stick is to go out into the country and hunt about for a suitable branch. Having found one, you cut it, bring it home, and attend to the finishing touches at leisure. In following this plan, it is highly important to see that no unnecessary damage is done to trees and bushes. Unless the branch can be selected without spoliation, it is far better to leave the work alone.

The proper time of the year for walking-stick making is in the autumn,

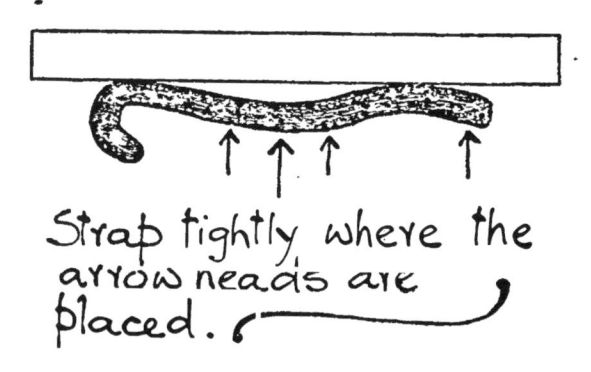

Strap tightly where the arrow heads are placed.

when the sap has descended. Choose a branch that is as straight as possible, and bear in mind that, usually, it must be peeled. Think, therefore, of the thickness, after peeling, and the length, when a handle has been provided and the tapering end cut off.

Having secured two or three branches that seem to be what you require, take them home and set to work on them. First trim off the rough parts, then examine them for straightness. It is, usually, found that a stick, when tested, is not nearly so erect as was, at first, supposed. Accordingly something must generally be done to straighten it. A good deal can be effected by holding the curved part in the steam of a kettle for some minutes and then forcing out the bend. Afterwards, the branch should be strapped tightly to a straight strip of wood and left for a fortnight. As the drying proceeds, the stick will harden and assume a straight line. If a natural curve was not obtained for the handle, it is possible to bend the end to the required shape while the steam-process is being carried out. It must, of course, be strapped, too.

When the stick has hardened, the finishing touches should be provided. Excrescences are easily removed by means of a spoke-shave, sand-paper will clean up the surfaces, and a good hard-drying varnish will add a suitable finish.

A TOBOGGAN YOU CAN MAKE

Undoubtedly, a thick carpet of snow covering the roads, the hill-sides and the meadows, is attractive, and as it is very fleeting, we must be ready for it so that the moment it arrives we may enjoy it to the full.

One of the things we shall certainly want for the next heavy fall of snow is a toboggan. Even though the sun may be scorchingly hot while you read these lines, it would not be a bad idea to set to work and make one. It will be ready and waiting for the time when freezing point is reached. You will only have, then, to get it out of the box-room, to put on a scarf and thick gloves and dash off along the shiny roads to the nearest hill-side.

There are many forms of toboggans, but the simplest of all to make is a mere platform set on runners. Two runners, each 3 feet long, 6 inches

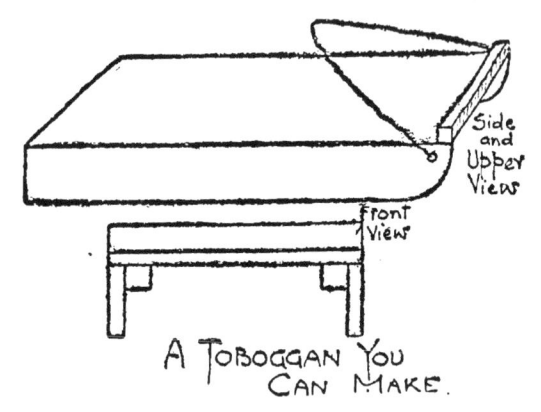

A TOBOGGAN YOU CAN MAKE.

wide, and an inch thick, will be required; also, enough floor boarding to cover the space between the runners, which should be about 3 by 2 feet. The runners are set up on edge and the floor boards are nailed across to form a platform. The front end of each runner should be curved on the bottom angle. A piece of rope must be threaded through holes in the front, for you to hold on to while rushing through the air, and also to drag it along by.

If you are keen on having a really good and useful toboggan, make one with a larger platform than the above, and erect a low seat on it. But be careful to note that the lower you sit, the less chance there is of you toppling over, and the less you will be hurt if you do capsize.

Some toboggans are fitted with a kind of brake. It is a long piece of wood which works on a central pin. One half projects above the platform, the other below it. By tugging the top half towards you, the lower half drags on the ground and slows down the speed. Note this, however: the brake must act in the centre of the toboggan; if it is at the side, the vehicle will skid round. Also, it must act well to the rear. If near the front, you will probably turn a somersault.

MAKING A DOOR

In many of the carpentry jobs which handy-boys undertake, such as making a shed or erecting a fence, a door proves to be the hardest part

Hundreds of Things a Boy Can Make

of the task. Now, unless the door is well constructed, is strong, serviceable and fits properly, the whole of the labour is more or less wasted. Accordingly, we propose to give here some useful hints on how one should be made.

In the first place, it is well to mention that, whenever possible, the side of the shed should be constructed to fit round the door rather than the door should be made to fit a given opening. If this is arranged, the width of the door can be made to equal the width of a certain number of pieces of wood: but, if the door has to fit a definite opening, it is almost sure to happen that one of the strips must be cut lengthwise and this provides a certain amount of weakness.

The wood required for the work may be purchased in various forms.

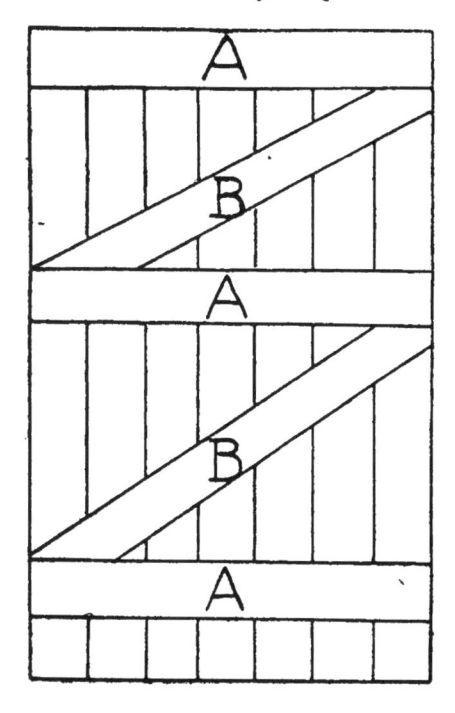

It may be square-edged boards, which will be merely arranged in planks, side by side. Tongued and grooved flooring, as its name implies, has a projection running along one edge and a recess along the other. Thus, one length fits into the next and, thereby, gains a good deal of strength. The two extreme edges of the door must be planed level, in this case, and, when measuring up, the fact should be remembered. Jointed matchboarding is similarly provided with edges which mesh together, but the wood, itself, is generally much thinner than the flooring just mentioned. Of these and the other classes of wood which the timber merchant can supply, either tongued and grooved flooring or jointed matchboarding will, probably, serve best.

Having purchased the wood, the next thing will be to cut it into the required vertical lengths. Most people, who wish to make a very good job of their work, will elect to cut each length an inch or two longer than the door is required to be. Then, when the pieces are assembled, each horizontal edge is marked with a pencil line and cut in one strip.

When all the pieces have been cut roughly to size, they are assembled on a level surface, such as the concrete floor of the back yard, and cross battens are nailed to them. Three horizontal crosspieces are required, one to fit along the top of the door, one not quite along the bottom, and the remaining one to run across the middle. (See A in the diagram.)

When these are fixed, two strips known as " braces " are needed to prevent the sagging and warping of the wood. These are marked B in the diagram. The ends of these pieces are awkwardly shaped, but no difficulty will be found in cutting them, if the wood is laid in position over the horizontal strips and pencil marks are made to show where the cutting is to be done.

Note that, where each of these five strips overlaps one of the original pieces, at least one nail should be driven in.

This being done, the door is planed along the vertical edges and sawn to exact requirements on the horizontal edges.

The next thing is to fit the door in position. This is a rather awkward task, but if somebody will come and give a hand, it is much easier. The door should be stood upright where it is to be fixed finally and, while the assistant is holding it, the uprights and crosspiece, surrounding the door, are fitted. In fixing them, it is well to remember that they must not come in actual contact with the edges of the door, but that there must be a gap of at least a quarter of an inch, more if the door is made of very thick wood. Unless the surrounding strips provide this gap, the door will refuse to open. Note, also, that the door must be raised a slight amount off the floor. If it actually stands on the ground, it will be impossible to move it.

Having fixed the frame around the door, the latter may be taken from its position temporarily, and projecting strips are then nailed on to the inside of the frame. This is done so that the door cannot push too far inwards and crack the hinges. It is presumed that it opens outwards. Three strips only are wanted, as should one be put behind the post which supports the hinged side of the door, the door will be prevented from swinging outwards.

All that remains is to fit the hinges and a lock, or catch. Before putting on the hinges, make up your mind how the door will open and put them on accordingly. The easiest way is to erect the door in a shut position, to open the hinges and to screw them flat on to the wood. When it is not desirable that the hinges should show, they must be fixed to the thickness of the door and to the inner edge of the post. The fitting of the lock calls for no particular mention.

TRY YOUR SKILL

Find an empty cardboard box about 10 inches high and the same number of inches wide and long. Then in one side cut out a round hole about three inches in diameter, a trifle nearer the top edge than the bottom. When that is done, ornament the outer faces of the box with various jazz colours, just to make it attractive.

Now divide the bottom of the box into about six compartments by fitting across it low strips of upstanding cardboard. Number each compartment with a figure—0, 5, 10, 15, etc.

In this simple manner you have provided yourself with a game that will give you hours of fun. Hand each player three pith balls—pellets of paper will do equally well; but see that each player can be identified

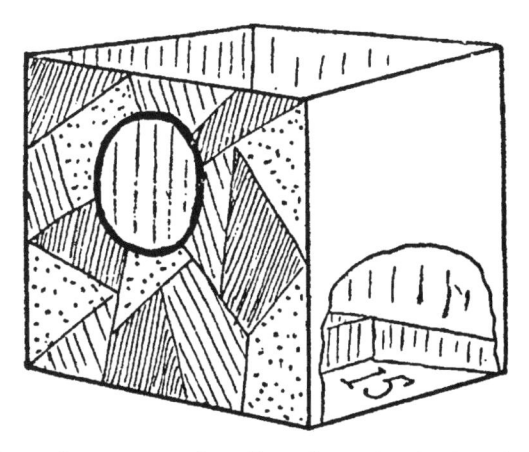

by a particular colour or mark. Stand twelve inches from the box and try to toss the balls through the opening. According to which compartment a ball falls into, so that number is added to the player's score. See who reaches fifty first.

A SEE-SAW

You can get a good deal of fun out of an improvised see-saw, made by resting a plank on a barrel; but it is far better to use a well made trestle for balancing the plank.

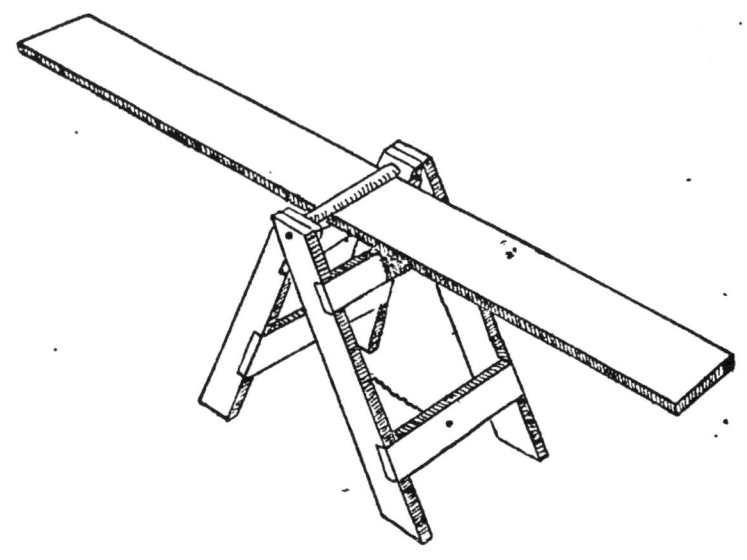

In the above diagram, a safe arrangement is shown, since the plank cannot slip off the fulcrum support, nor can it tip up too high, owing to the provision of a stop-bar.

As you will, probably, make this see-saw from improvised pieces of wood, it will be useless to give actual dimensions. All that need be said is that the legs of the trestle should be about 4 feet long and that two horizontals should be fixed across each pair of supporting strips. Note that in the diagram, the further side of the trestle fits into the nearer side, at the top junction. Accordingly, the cross bars for the further side of the trestle are slightly shorter than those required for the nearer side.

Do not place the two upper bars too high up on the faces of the trestle. If you were to fix them right at the top, the plank would be unable to rise and fall; and, if you were to put them very low down one end of the plank would bump clumsily on the ground. Thus, you must decide on an intermediate position. About 6 inches below the stop-bar will, probably, serve best.

The plank should be from three to four times the length of the trestle legs.

THE NUMBERED BOARD

Do you like games of skill? If so, here is something you will be sure to make. It is a board for hanging on the wall. On the board are the numbers one to twelve, and above each number is a hook. Competitors are given three rubber rings and told to stand 6 feet away—a lesser distance for those under ten. The game is to score the highest number of points. It is a splendid way to pass a wet afternoon.

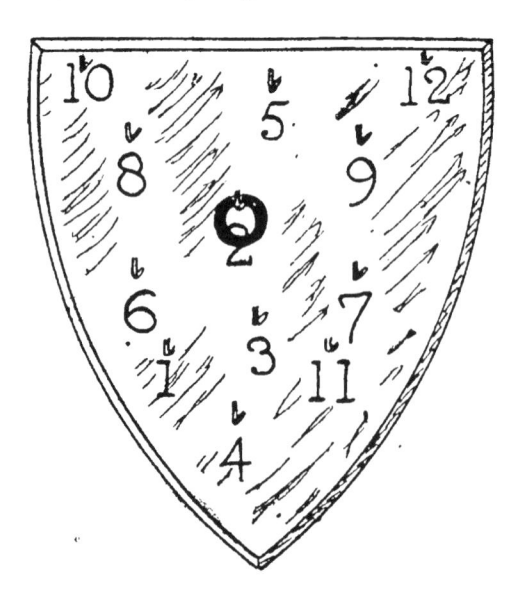

To make the board, get a piece of wood, large enough to enable you to cut out of it a shield shape 2 feet high and 18 inches wide. Some of the wood sold for fret-work purposes answers admirably. Three-ply wood is not quite thick enough to take the hooks and should only be used if nothing better can be obtained. Decide on a V-shaped board if you must do the cutting with an ordinary saw; but should a fret-saw or a key-hole saw be available, make the sides curved like those of an ordinary shield. Trim the edges nicely and then give two coats of a bright-coloured cellulose paint. It will be quite hard and dry in a few hours.

Now space the figures equally on the board, putting the low numbers in the centre and the high ones at the edges—just to make scoring a little difficult. Above each number screw in a dresser hook, and then put in another hook so that the board may be hung on the wall.

The rubber rings which we use did duty in their early life round the stoppers of pickle-jars.

A DART BOARD

Have you ever played at darts? It is a fine game to test your aim, and the necessary board is easily constructed.

You will want a circle about 18 inches to 2 feet in diameter, made of some "spongy" material, so that the darts will easily stick into it. A soft, open-grained wood will do, or, failing this, use a thin piece of any wood and glue on to it a facing of cork lino. Paint the surface and draw a dozen radii, or spokes, and in the spaces so formed print the numbers one to twelve. Put a loop on the back of the wood, to hang it by, and the board is finished.

Be very careful that no aim is taken while anyone is standing by the side of the board, and it is a good plan to make a rule that a dart must not be thrown until all spectators are situated in the rear of the player.

Make the darts by forcing half a knitting needle into a pear-shaped piece of cork, sharpening the tip. If a feathered end is fitted the flight of the dart will be more true.

A CHEAP PERISCOPE

A periscope is a very useful thing for enabling you to look over the top of a high wall, round a corner or into other inaccessible places. To our soldiers, in the late war, it was, of course, a great boon, because it gave them opportunities of seeing without being seen.

A periscope is nothing more than a long narrow box, with two openings, and a mirror at each end. From this, it is clear that it should not be a difficult task to make one.

The actual dimensions of the contrivance do not matter, but having made and used several periscopes, we consider that the length of the box should be about 20 inches and 2 inches for the other measurements.

Thus a piece of card 20 inches long and 9 inches wide is wanted. The width will have to be divided into four portions each of 2 inches and the remaining inch is required for lapping the joins, when the card is folded to form a long rectangular figure. This figure, it should be said, will have the two small ends open; but they will be closed by pasting a square of cardboard in position, when all else is finished.

When the large piece of card has been trimmed to shape, but before it is folded and joined up, it is necessary to cut two small windows in it. One must be at what is designed to be the top and the other at the bottom; but the top window should come in the front face, and the bottom in the back face.

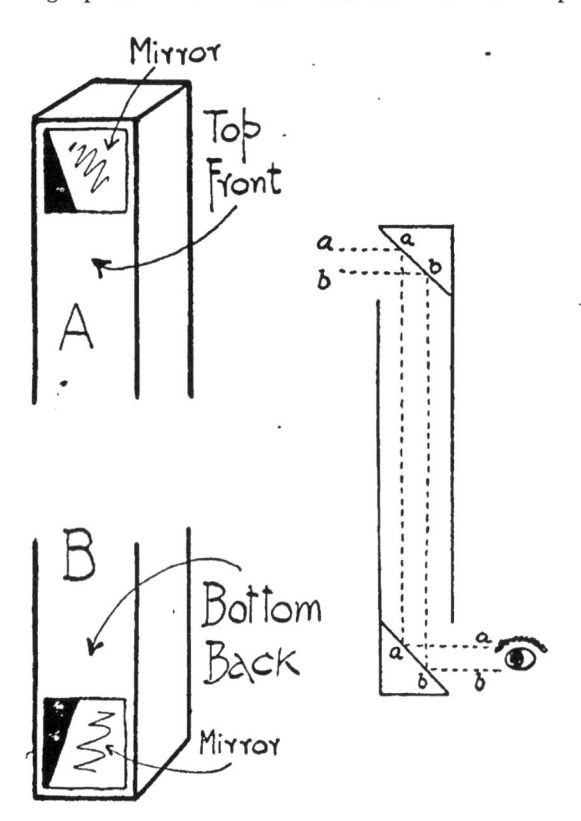

Two small pieces of mirror are needed; they must both be the same size. One of the pieces is pasted inside the top of the rectangle, as shown at A, and the other, at the bottom of the rectangle, as shown at B. It is very important that both should be fixed at an angle of 45 degrees with the top and the bottom faces, respectively. This can be done, conveniently, by pasting strips of passe-partout binding to the mirror and to the inside face of the rectangle. The mirrors will need to be 2 inches wide, or perhaps a fraction of an inch less; but just how long they are required is a difficult matter to calculate. The best plan, therefore, is to fit two dummy pieces of card, and, when they have been cut exactly to the required size, to procure the mirrors with similar dimensions.

Before closing up the rectangle and finishing it off, it is advisable to coat the whole of the inside faces of the cardboard with black ink. This will check any glare that may otherwise be thrown on to the mirrors.

Diagram C shows how the periscope works. An object AB, is sighted through the top window. It is reflected on to the slanting mirror, seen above, and deflected through the length of the rectangle to the bottom mirror. There it is reflected through the bottom window to your eyes, which are stationed close to the opening on the right.

THE STURDY STEED

What do you think of this atrocious steed? It is simply terrible, isn't it? Yet you will agree that it is just the thing for a fancy dress party, a carnival, or other function of merriment. It will cause roars of laughter wherever it goes.

And, the best of it all is that you can make it in a few hours out of all sorts of odds and ends.

The picture will reveal to you a good deal of the construction. First, you will need a fancy dress costume, such as that of a clown, a pierrot, or something else grotesque. Have a frill around your waist to hide the join where you fit into the frisky steed.

Begin by constructing the body framework. A length of stout cane will serve admirably for the curved horizontal rib, and the dome-shaped rib attached to it. Be very careful that you make all joins extra strong, otherwise, when you become frisky, they may work loose and fly out, with sad consequences.

62 *Hundreds of Things a Boy Can Make*

This done, shape the head and shoulders out of woolly cloth. Sew the pieces together on the wrong side, turn inside out and stuff with paper. Don't forget to provide two loppy ears, and a couple of startling eyes. Fix all this tightly on to the cane frame. Then drape the frame to make the body and leg covering. The height of this latter covering must be equal to your measurement from waist to ankle.

All sorts of funny trappings may be added at will, but do not forget to put on a leg, on either side, to imitate your own real legs.

The above particulars will complete all the necessary requirements, but if you are handy at fitting electrical devices, we suggest that one eye of the steed should be made to contain an electric bulb, attached to a battery fixed on the frame, and joined up by a length of wire running through the padded head. A hidden switch will enable you to make the creature wink just when you feel it ought. Also, have a string running through the tail, so that, on giving it a tug, this part of the anatomy jumps about.

A TRIMMING DEVICE FOR SNAPSHOTS

It is very seldom that a snapshot does not require trimming and, if you want to make a picture of your print, it is generally necessary to cut away a good deal of the edges, so that the eye shall not be led away from the chief points of interest.

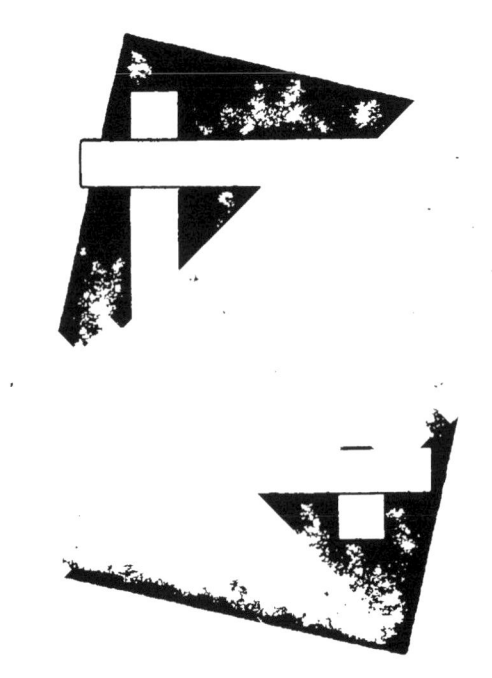

It is not easy for a person who is not a trained artist to decide, by a mere glance, which part of a print should be retained in order to secure the best effect. The two pieces of white card, cut to the shape of the letter L and shown in the diagram, will however tell the novice, quickly, how he should trim his prints.

Hundreds of Things a Boy Can Make

The two pieces of card must be in the form of right angles. They may be conveniently made out of a stiff postcard.

To use them, put them on the print, as shown, and move them about, square with each other, until a pleasing picture is obtained within the white margins.

A TOY FORT

A toy fort provides lots of fun if you have an army of tin soldiers with one or two guns on wheels. The best material with which to make it is thin fretwood for the frame, and whitening mixed with glue for the moulded parts.

A simple design is given as a pattern, but it may be altered, of course, if desired. If the present design is followed the frontage should be about 15 inches long and the total height about a foot. Although the frontage suggests a square building, the remaining three sides need not be added unless a store place is required for the miniature army.

In front of the building is a terrace 3 inches wide, and then comes a castellated wall with an inclined roadway running down to the level of the surrounding land.

When the pieces of wood have been cut with a fret-saw and nailed together some whitening is mixed with hot glue and spread over the parts that are required to be unevenly modelled, such as the grassy embankments at the side of the sloping roadway.

The last stage is the colouring, which may be done readily with oils or paints of the cellulose type.

A TOY ENGINE

Toy wooden engines are just the things which some children appreciate, especially if couplings are provided, so that all manner of rolling, and even non-rolling stock, may be tied behind, and the whole calvacade drawn along in procession by means of a string in the front. Therefore, set to work and make one of these pleasure-giving toys; some kiddie or other will be grateful to you.

First of all, decide on the base-board. A piece of wood, ¾ inch thick and 14 inches long by 5 inches wide, will provide a comfortable size. Square this piece carefully, and smooth all the edges so that small hands will not be damaged by splinters. Then commence to erect the body-work.

The boiler should be considered first of all. Being round in section, it will not be easy to shape unless you have access to a lathe. But a very creditable result can be obtained by using a chisel and so rounding the edges of a piece of square sectioned wood, 4 inches along each side. You will want it about 7 inches long. Remember to flatten

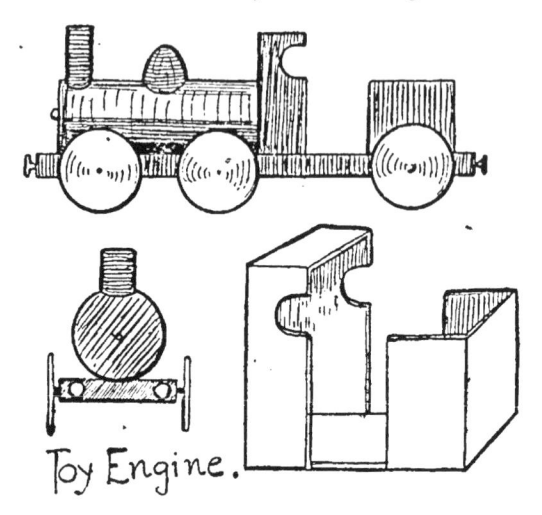

Toy Engine.

a portion of the circumference so that the boiler will lie snugly on the base-board. We have more than once overcome the difficulty of shaping the boiler out of wood by using a piece of millboard tubing, and fitting a round of thin wood to stop up the opening at the front. If a stout tube is selected, it will be just as serviceable as solid wood and far less heavy.

Before actually fixing the boiler, it will be well to make the funnel and the steam-chamber. These should be cut out of round rods—a broom-handle will do—and shaped as required. If fitted into wood, a slight recess is all that is needed, but if a millboard tube is used, it is best to run the two fittings down to the chassis, and pin them from underneath.

The next thing is to cut out and fit the cab. Make the upright piece 6 inches high, 2 inches long, and as wide as the chassis, that is 5 inches. If you have the necessary implements, cut out on both sides a half circle to serve as a "look-out." The back tender will be about correct if made 4 inches high, and reaching to the end of the base-board.

You will now want three axles. Strips of wood an inch square in section and 6 inches long will be suitable. Fix them where the wheels are to be fitted, as shown in the diagram.

Six wheels are required. As metal ones can be bought very cheaply, it is a waste of time and energy to try to make them of wood, unless

Hundreds of Things a Boy Can Make

a lathe is at hand. Fix them to the axle ends by means of stout screws. All the rest of the fixing of the various parts should be done with panel pins that will not split the wood.

This toy will please the kiddies far more if painted with bright colours, than if left in the white. Give the body a coat of vivid green, paint the funnel black, the steam chamber yellow, and the buffer ends red.

The last thing is to fix little brass knobs, such as people use for curtain strings, to serve as the buffers and then put accurately in the centre of the front end of the boiler a hook to take a piece of string. Another hook might be fixed in the centre of the back buffer plate.

A SELF-PROPELLED SHIP

That little boat of yours, which you sail on the park lake, can be made to rip through the water like the fastest cutter if it is fitted with the apparatus described below.

First cut out the slot A from the stern of the boat and nail sheet brass around it, on both sides, as shown by the shaded lines. Let the brass, which should be in one piece, come a trifle below the original keel line,

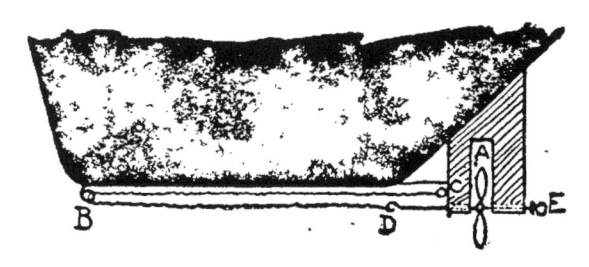

and, in the space so formed run a stout rod carrying a propeller to fit into the space A. At the end of the rod E place a washer and a ring handle; also a loop at D.

Now fix a screw eye at B, another at C, and run from C, through B to D, a length of ¼ inch square-faced rubber. Tie it strongly to the ends.

When all is ready, twist the handle at E and knot up the rubber fully along its entire length. Place the boat in the water, while still gripping the handle; then let go and away whizzes the craft at a most exciting rate. Set the rudder so that the course brings the craft back home.

A LIFEBUOY

Do you spend much of your time in or upon the water—boating, swimming, skating, etc? If so, this lifebuoy should be of interest to you.

Get an old cover of a motor tyre and, then, save up a number of empty cylindrical tins which have press-on lids fitted to them. All the tins should be the same size and their circular measurement should be suited to the inner curve of the tyre. They must not be too large, for instance, to fit inside the cover, nor yet so small as to slip about freely. It will not matter, however, if they are just a trifle small, because, as will be seen, that can be rectified.

When you have a number of tins, fit them inside the cover, end to end, to complete the circle and, then, make several holes, with a bradawl, in both edges of the cover and lace them tightly together.

You now have a very serviceable lifebuoy.

Before putting the tins in position, remember to hit each lid with a hammer to keep it from coming off.

THE WATER CUTTER

Everybody likes playing with water, so this little device will find a good deal of favour. To make it you will want a round disc of tin about 3 or 4 inches in diameter. Just the thing for the purpose is the circle of thin metal which has to be cut out of the barrel-shaped tins of fifty cigarettes before they can be opened. Of course the material can be derived from numbers of other sources.

When you have a suitable disc, cut saw-like teeth all round the edge. They need to be fairly well indented. Then pencil a diameter across the metal, divide its length into three approximately equal parts, and where the two marks come, punch two holes. If you have no suitable tool for making the holes, place the metal upon a piece of waste wood—not on the mahogany dining-room table!—and hammer two stout nails through. Pull the nails out and you have two holes that will do quite well.

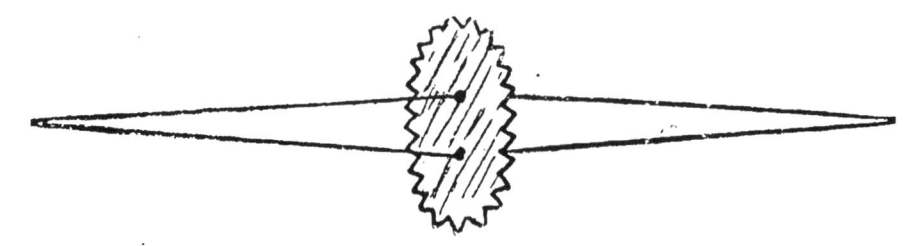

Now thread a piece of string through the holes, as shown in the illustration, and the water cutter is finished.

To use it, hold the two tips of the string almost taut and jerk the disc round and round until the two lengths of string have become much twisted; then give them a little jerk in the opposite direction and round the wheel will spin like lightning. As it revolves, let it just touch the surface of a bowl of water and up flies the water in an alarming way.

If, whenever the string has almost unwound itself, the two ends are smartly brought a trifle closer together and then, equally smartly, carried out to their full extent again, the wheel will continue to spin indefinitely. But note carefully that this action causes the wheel to rotate first in one direction and then the other. Accordingly, the water will fly up both away from you and towards you ; so, unless you raise it above the surface when its direction is towards you, you will get well splashed. Of course the greatest fun is to rotate it when you are in your bath ; then, it will not matter if you do get wet.

A BOW AND ARROW

Some boys would not feel that they had lived if they had not made a bow and some arrows. So here are a few hints. First, get a nice length of supple wood. If you have a choice pick a yew twig, or, failing that, a nice whippy piece of willow or ash. Your strip should be about 5 feet long ; it must be smooth throughout, and there ought not to be much difference in the stoutness between either end. The wood being selected, rub it smooth all over with fine glass-paper and round off the two tips. Now cut a notch, 3 inches off both ends, but do not let the grooves be so deep as to weaken the tips. At the centre of the wood glue a soft piece of velvet so that it binds round the bow—it should be about 6 inches wide. The next thing is to fix the cord. If you want to make a really good job get a length of ong cord, uch as anglers use for their fishing lines, and, if it is a little too thin, plait two lengths firmly together. Now run three turns of the cord round one of the notched ends, and tie it firmly. Next tie up the remaining end, but only do it temporarily. Then test the pull of the bow. If it seems to have a good healthy spring, due to a sufficient arching of the wood, go ahead with the tying, and make the second end a fixture. If it has not, bend the wood a little more.

And now as to the arrows. Any straight and stout twigs, 3 feet long, will do nicely. Point them at the tips, and split the tails, fixing in the splits the feathery part of goose quills. Glue up the splits. Do not spend too much time on the arrows, however, as you will constantly be losing and breaking them, and the trouble is not worth while.

Use your bow in the open, not where people are likely to be struck by the arrows. If you are careful you will have a fine instrument, but if you are careless it will be a source of danger.

TO PROVE THAT IRON EXPANDS WHEN HEATED

This capital experiment may be performed easily by you if you have learnt to solder. You will want a thin flat bar of iron, a Bunsen burner, and a steel knitting needle.

First take the needle, and to one end solder a 4 inch length of wire. If you have fixed it with an ugly " blob " of solder, file away the lumpy part so as to provide a neat join. Now bend the wire at right angles to the needle.

Take two fairly large boxes of equal size, stand them on a table, place the bar of iron on the top and so form a bridge. But be careful of one thing, the iron must overlap the boxes at least 2 inches at either end ; more, if possible. On one end of the iron, stand all the weights you can borrow from the kitchen scales. Put nothing on the other end, but place the knitting needle under it to act as a roller, and see, that, the bar does not drag on the surface of the box anywhere. Now set the Bunsen going under the centre of the bar, which will soon become heated.

68   *Hundreds of Things a Boy Can Make*

As the iron warms up, the wire indicator attached to the needle will begin to describe an arc of a circle. This is because the iron is expanding. It cannot move along where the weights are put; they are pegging it down. So it pushes along at the other end, and its weight rolls the knitting needle over. The movement may be slight, but the wire exaggerates it, and this latter contrivance can be seen to turn an appreciable amount. If a little paper dial, shaped as a half circle, is placed upright behind the indicator, it is possible to make some sort of measurement relative to the expansion of the bar.

We have no room for further experiments, but many suggestions for others will be found in lesson books dealing with Physics, Heat, Light and Sound, and Chemistry. If you learn nothing else from them, you will soon find out that these books are really interesting, and not the dull things some folk think they are.

A BROOM RACK

A broom rack for the scullery is a very useful article, yet it is not difficult to make. You will require two pieces of wood, each 3½ feet long, and three pieces, each about 3 feet long. The wood should be about 5 inches wide and 1 inch thick.

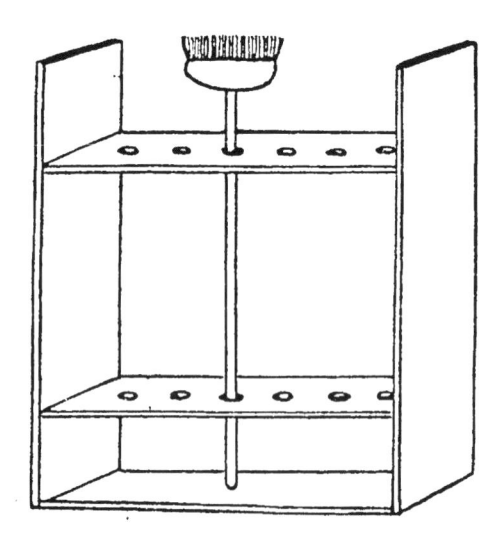

In cutting the wood to its exact lengths, be careful to saw along lines that are made square by means of an L piece or a set-square. If you guess at the lines, they will not fit together accurately and, when finished, the rack will wobble.

The two long pieces of wood are required for the uprights and the shorter lengths for the floor of the rack and the two perforated shelves. For assembling the various pieces, use 2 inch wire nails.

Before the rack is put together, make the necessary holes in the two shelves by means of a brace and bit or, failing the possession of this tool, it is not difficult to burn them out with a red-hot poker. Make all the holes in one plank first; then put the perforated plank on the other one, mark the position of the holes through it, on to the other.

In this way, it is a simple matter to get the corresponding holes one above the other.

When all the fixing is done, give the wood a coat of stain or paint.

SWAT THAT FLY !

If, for one day, we could follow a fly in its travels from place to place, it is very certain that we should never give these pests any quarter again. We should be devising all sorts of ways of encompassing their extermination.

Although there are countless forms of fly-catchers, few compare in point of efficiency with the short sharp method of swatting them.

To make a first-rate swatter, with plenty of life in it, obtain a flat lath, 8 inches long, 1 inch wide and ½ inch thick. Then, hunt about for a piece of old cycle inner tubing. A piece about 6 inches square is needed. Spread it out flat and nail it to the wood, as shown in the diagram. Note that a piece of tape has been fixed between the nail-heads and the rubber. This is to prevent the heads cracking the rubber.

AN EXPANDING TOY

This is just the sort of plaything that will amuse many youngsters for hours. You will see what to aim at by looking at the diagram. Eight pieces of wood, 4 inches long and an inch wide, will be required. The material can be bought in long laths from the wood-yard or strip wood will serve. In addition two pieces of wood 5 inches long are needed for the handles. They must be 2 inches in width at the wider end and taper down to 1 inch at the narrower end. These will have to be cut and trimmed out of a piece of box-lid or similar material. At the wider end a round hole must be cut, large enough to allow a finger to be slipped through.

Now let the pieces be assembled. First arrange them as suggested by the diagram ; then prick holes at the ends with a fine awl and push panel pins through the wood, so as to join up the two thicknesses at each corner. Turn over the projecting part of each pin and snip off all but sufficient to hold the wood.

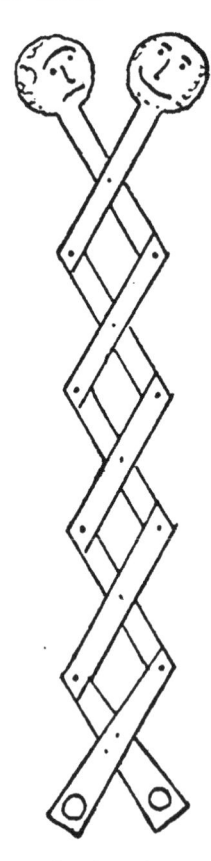

At the far end, away from the handles, nail on two grotesque faces, cut out of stiff cardboard and coloured with pen and brush.

To use, place a finger and thumb through the two holes in the handles. Contract the hand and the lattice arrangement springs out its full length. Expand the hand and the lattice draws in. It is capital fun.

Note that if a number of these toys are to be made—say for selling at a bazaar or a Boy Scouts' sale of work—much labour can be saved by using garden lattice-work for the square parts.

Colour all the wood with some bright, quick-drying paint.

AN AIR PRESSURE EXPERIMENT

A piece of apparatus, which is easily put together, is the following : Obtain an empty two pound glass jam jar, and cut a cork to fit it exactly. In passing, it may be said that the young scientist will find a supply of sheet cork very useful for various purposes; preferably, it should be an inch thick. In the cork, bore two holes, one to take a glass funnel, and the other an elbow joint of glass tubing. If the fitting of the jar, the funnel, or the tubing, has not been done perfectly, run sealing wax round the joins in order to make them air-tight.

When all is ready, place your finger over the outside end of the elbow joint of glass, and then fill the funnel with water. Nothing happens. The water stays in the funnel. Now, take your finger away from the glass tube, and immediately the water rushes from the funnel down into the jar. Why? In the first case, the jar was filled with air and its pressure kept the water high up in the funnel, but the moment your finger was taken away, the water pushed the air out of the jar, up through the tube and into the room. This is, of course, a little experiment to prove that air exerts a constant pressure.

AN ELECTRIC BELL

The making of an electric bell from odd pieces of metal, wood and other substances is not an exceedingly difficult matter. Any mechanically minded boy can do it with a little care, if he will study the accompanying diagram and follow the explanation of how the bell works.

The rectangle, shown in the illustration, is a piece of hard wood and the dotted shape is an iron plate. A and P are the two terminals of the bell and the two installation wires from the battery and the push run one to each. The current enters through A and leaves at B. From A, it travels along the coil of wire B, and continues on, reaching one of the two reels around which is wound many turns of green-silk-covered wire. The silk covering acts as an insulator and so insulates all the turns of wire on the reel from one another, forcing the current to travel the whole length of the turns. The end of this wire should be bared and twisted to the bared end of the windings of the second reel, and so the current goes on through the second reel, along the coil C to D. D is a screw which bites the wire C down to the bottom iron plate.

It is now clear that there is an electrical path from A to anywhere on the bottom iron plate. E is a piece of metal which stands up from the bottom plate and is in electrical contact with it. To E is bolted a piece of flat steel spring, F G. To this spring is also bolted a piece of soft iron, H. It will be seen now that current can travel from A to G. L is a pillar, in contact with M and P, but L and M are slightly raised and do not touch the bottom plate. J (regulated by the brass head, K) is a screw through M, and it just touches the spring G, thereby completing the path from A to P.

When the bell push is operated, a current runs from A to P and it has to traverse the many turn on both reels. Down the centre of each reel is a soft iron rod or core—the ends of them can be seen in the diagram. As soon as the many turns of wire carry current, these soft iron cores behave as powerful magnets. The instant the flow of current ceases in those turns the cores lose all their magnetic power.

As soon as current is passed, the magnetized cores pull the soft iron, H, to them, overcoming the spring action of F. But note what has now happened; if H is drawn to the reels, the portion of the spring GF, which touched J, becomes drawn away from it. If J and the spring,

72 *Hundreds of Things a Boy Can Make*

GF, are not in contact, no current can pass from A to P. Therefore, all current ceases in the turns of the wire on the reels, the cores of the reels lose their magnetic powers and are unable to attract H. The spring, F, then causes H to fly back to its original position, when GF will again touch J. Instantly, the path for a current from A to P is restored. At once, H flies to the cores, breaking contact between GF and J. Current is again cut off, to be restored immediately. This goes on as long as the push-button is pressed.

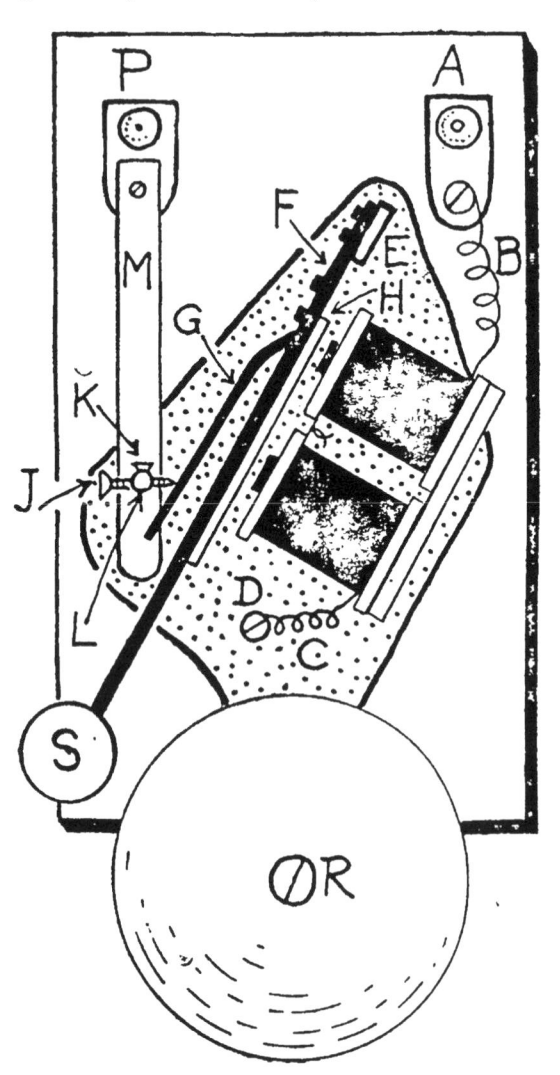

So far, we have not noticed the bell R, or the clapper S. The shank of the clapper is fixed to the soft iron H, and is so adjusted that the knob, S, is brought with a smart tap against the rim of the bell, whenever H is drawn to the iron cores. Just as the hammer reaches the gong, GF has left J, so that the current no longer flows from A to P, and the striker instantly rebounds from the gong.

Hundreds of Things a Boy Can Make

For the gong, you will probably be able to use part of an old bicycle bell; for the flat steel spring, a strip of spring from a broken mechanical toy; odd bits of metal will serve for most of the other parts; but for the green silk-covered wire it is best to buy new material. It is extremely cheap, however.

AN ELECTRIC BURGLAR ALARM

Burglar alarms are very useful devices to install in the home. They serve a double purpose, for, not only do they warn the householder that his premises are in danger, but, what is still more useful, they usually frighten the burglar and cause him to retreat before he does any considerable amount of damage.

Alarms may be arranged according to several different plans. One idea is to wire the premises so that, when a door or window is opened, the circuit is completed and the bell rings; but a much better plan is

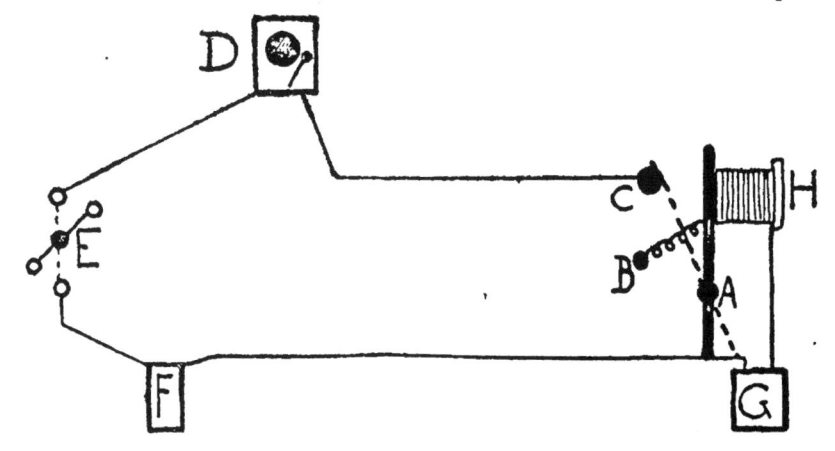

to arrange the wiring so that, when doors or windows are moved, the main circuit is broken and a smaller circuit is formed which sets the bell in motion. This is the better arrangement because the alarm does not cease when a burglar cuts the wire or quickly closes a door behind him; it goes on until the householder re-sets the whole arrangement.

A suitable lay-out for wiring according to this plan is shown in the diagram. It will be see that the following parts are needed: an alarm bell, a dry battery, a gravity battery, an electro-magnet, a switch, a supply of fine covered wire and various small fittings.

In setting up such a system, it will be advisable to commence at the points of entry to the house—in other words, at the doors and windows.

A small plate of copper is fitted to the hinged edge of each door, and a corresponding plate to the fixed wooden upright adjacent to it. The two plates must be in electrical contact, when the door is closed. Since such an arrangement can sometimes complicate the legitimate movement of the door, it may be necessary to fit, to the fixed strip of wood, a plate provided with a projecting disc. Behind the disc is a spring which enables the disc to shoot out or press inwards; thus, proper contact is always obtained. A fitting of this kind can be bought for less than sixpence. With regard to casement windows, they are, of course, treated in the same manner as doors; while sash windows require the two plates to be fitted one on the sill and the other on the sliding frame.

The plates being fixed, they are connected up to a circuit formed of thin covered wire. An examination of the diagram will show that the lay-out very much resembles that generally used for an electric door bell. There is, for instance, the electro magnet, which attracts a thin metal plate. This plate can revolve about the point, A; also, it is held by a spring, B, but the attractive force of the magnet must be greater than that of the spring, while the current is passing.

The working of the circuit may be explained, as follows:

In the daytime, when no check is needed, the switch E is put in the "off" position and no current passes. The circuit is, in fact, dead.

At night or when the house is left, the switch E is put in the "on" position to join up the wires. It will be seen that there is still a gap in that part of the circuit containing the bell, and, of course, it does not ring. But should the connection be broken by the opening of a door between the gravity cell and the electro-magnet, the latter loses its power, the attraction on the revolving plate, A, is lost and the spring, B, pulls the plate to C. This completes the bell circuit and the ringing commences.

A burglar can do nothing to stop the alarm, because the only way to silence it is to push the arm of A back to the magnet, when all doors and windows have been once more closed; and, of course the burglar does not know where to find the magnet.

There is very little in this alarm system to get out of order, but the batteries must, of course, be attended to regularly.

WATERPROOFING MATCHES

If you are fond of picnics on the river, as we are, you have probably found that, somehow or other, the matches for lighting the spirit kettle always seem to get damp and refuse to light. It is really a very serious matter when this happens, because, however much you may want a cup of tea, it is denied you. Of course, if men are among the party, things are different, because they seem to know how to keep matches dry.

Here is a way, however, to overcome the trouble. Before starting out, take the matches out of a box and dip the heads in some melted candle fat. Even if the box then falls into the water, the matches will strike easily enough.

A MARKETING BOARD

One of the most exacting duties of a housewife is to keep an eye on the kitchen supplies and to order fresh quantities when they are required. As a rule, she endeavours to work by memory; but it is a far better plan to have a tablet, hanging in a prominent place, and to mark on it the supplies that have to be purchased.

A very neat plan is to construct a marketing board, as shown in the illustration. All the usual commodities are printed on it in columns, and, by the side of each, a hole is made. When supplies of any article need replenishing, a peg is slipped into the appropriate hole. It then serves as a reminder when a shopping expedition is about to take place.

```
WANTED
○ Bacon        ○ Margarine
○ Biscuits     ○ Marmalade
○ Butter       ○ Matches
○ Candles      ○ Milk (Tin)
○ Cheese       ○ Mustard
○ Cocoa        ○ Paraffin
○ Coffee       ○ Pepper
○ Currants     ○ Raisins
○ Eggs         ○ Salt
○ Fish         ○ Soap
○ Flour        ○ Soda
○ Jam          ○ Sugar
○ Lard         ○ Tea
○ Library      ○ Vinegar
    Book
```

To construct the board, obtain two sheets of thin wood, about 10 by 8 inches. Draw up the list of commodities and print each name on one sheet of paper a trifle smaller than the pieces of wood.

When this is done, paste the paper to the wood and give it a coat of varnish. On drying, use a brace and bit to make a round hole by the side of each name, large enough to take a match stick.

The next thing is to nail a thin strip of wood along both the shorter edges of the back of the board and then to nail the second sheet of wood to the two thin strips. A hole is also made in the board by which it can be hung up.

The marketing board is now complete. Between the two faces, slip an envelope containing a number of dead matches. They will serve quite well as indicator pegs.

AN INVERTED ELECTRIC LIGHT SHADE

Eye specialists are becoming more and more convinced that many people have trouble with their sight because, in their homes, the electric light bulbs are not screened. Here is the way to make a shade that screens the bulb and which affords the necessary amount of rest and comfort required by the eyes.

Take a large piece of parchment paper or imitation vellum and draw a circle on it, about eighteen inches in diameter. Cut out the circle and, then, make a straight slit from anywhere on the circumference to the centre and, about an inch away from the slit, measuring on the circumference, make another slit to the centre. Remove the loose piece, which will be wedge-shaped, bring the two radii together, and glue them, one overlapping about an eighth of an inch on the other.

The circle of vellum is no longer flat but slightly conical. With the tip downwards, hold it up to the bulb for which it is intended. If it does not hide the direct rays, when viewed by a person walking about the room, it is advisable to cut a small piece more from the circle and

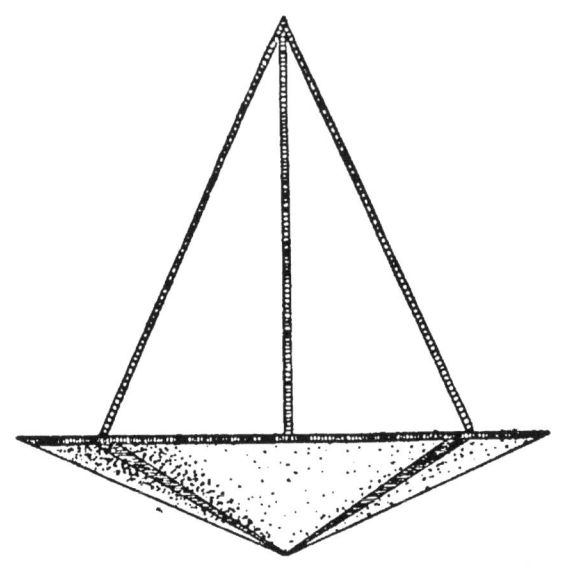

glue, as before. This will have the effect of raising the sides of the circle more than in the first case. We suggest this method of trial, because what suits one bulb may not suit another. The height of the light and other factors have to be considered.

Having made the shape, as desired, obtain some narrow gold braid and stick it all round the circular edge ; then put a strip over the radial join of the vellum to hide it, and place two more radial strips at equal distances, to match the first.

Where the three radial strips of braid meet the circumference, stick three long strips of braid, carry them up to a point above the bulb, and tie them to the electric flex.

MAKING THE POISON BOTTLES SAFE

Every now and again, the newspapers tell us about somebody who has drunk out of a poison bottle by mistake. Of course, it seems a silly thing to do, yet it is quite easily done in one of those moments when we are off our guard. The problem which various people have tried to solve is " how can a person have it impressed on his mind that he is handling a poison bottle ? " Many things have been suggested—blue bottles, ridged bottles, hexagonal-shaped bottles, and so on.

What we think is a very good idea is to cut strips of glass-paper and glue them to the neck of every bottle in the house, containing poison. The strips should reach up to the cork.

On gripping the cork of such a bottle, the roughness must be felt—it cannot be avoided, and it acts as an alarm signal. Of course, this

Glass Paper

POISON

idea is not intended to take the place of other precautions, but merely to supplement them.

A COAT HANGER IN THE SCULLERY

A penny coat-hanger can be as useful in the scullery as it is in the bedroom. Fit five or seven screwhooks to the carved wooden shoulder

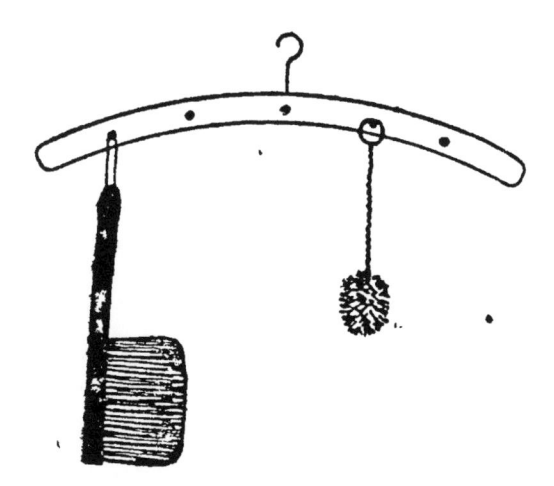

and hang it on a peg in the scullery. There, it will serve for supporting mops, short brooms, dust pans, cloths and a variety of other objects.

78   *Hundreds of Things a Boy Can Make*

More than likely when you have contrived one of these hangers, you will be asked to fit up two or three more. One can then be kept for brooms, and dust pans, another for dusters and cloths, another for washing apparatus, and so on. Articles of one nature will not foul those of another, then.

A USEFUL TIE PRESS

Every self-respecting boy values a tie press in these days, and as one can be made in an evening, there is no reason why you should be without this useful article. It will take out all those objectionable creases which make tying next time so difficult a matter.

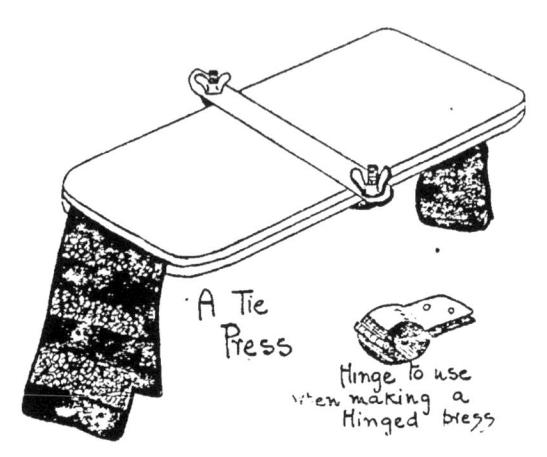

A Tie Press

Hinge to use when making a Hinged Press

You will want two pieces of wood, 10 inches long by 4 wide. If you have no suitable material at hand, the fretwork shops will be able to supply you. Buy an attractive kind of wood, such as satin walnut or ebony, and have it ¾ inch thick. Cut the two pieces exactly the same size, round off the edges neatly, and smooth the surfaces carefully with fine glass-paper.

The next thing is to determine how you will operate the press. There is a choice of ways. First, you can fix two hinges so that the pieces of wood open out like a book and are tightened by means of a clasp. For this you will want hinges that project well beyond the wooden edges, in order that they may not be strained when considerable pressure is applied.

A second way is to fit a cross bar of wood to both the top and bottom section. Let it be ¾ inch square in section, and allow a 1 inch projection at the ends to take the thumb screws for tightening up.

The third and best way is to use a metal cross bar, which is actuated by wing nuts, fixed to an under bridge of metal. If the latter method is adopted, it will be best to procure all the necessary metal parts from Handicrafts Ltd. for 1s. 6d., post free, the set. They are all nicely nickel-plated and serve to make the job a good one. Wait, of course, until you are in possession of these parts before cutting the wood, as it must be made to fit.

The finish given to the wood needs consideration. French polish is very effective.

A TROUSER HANGER MADE OF CLOTHES PEGS

Do you try to keep the crease in your trousers? Of course, a trouser-press is the best aid in this matter, but there is not always time to get out the press, fold your trousers neatly and screw up the boards.

When not in a press and not on your person, your trousers should be

folded and hung with the bottom part upwards. There is no better way of keeping them in shape.

To make three or four hangers, get twice as many clothes pegs—the kind which clips with a wire spring; put them 4 inches apart and join them by means of a stout piece of wire. Give the wire a curl in the middle, so that it will slip over a hook. You can make a hanger in four minutes at a cost of a halfpenny.

ORNAMENTING A CLOTHES-BRUSH

A very serviceable clothes-brush can be purchased for sixpence or a shilling, but it will not be a very attractive article. What you can very easily do, however, is to beautify it.

Take the brush and run over the wooden part with fine glass-paper. You should aim at smoothing down the rough places and also, at removing all shine on the surface.

This done, place the back of the brush on a sheet of drawing or note paper and run a pencil line round the edges. Then, cut out the shape.

Next, get out your box of paints and draw and colour a neat design on the paper. For this purpose, the best effects are secured by plenty of bright masses of colour and not by niggling detailed designs.

When the paints have thoroughly dried, stick the picture on the back of the brush and see that the edges lie perfectly flat. Then, run a strip

80   *Hundreds of Things a Boy Can Make*

of colour around the edges of the wood and leave the brush for at least a day.

The final step is to cover the picture and the coloured edge with a

coat of light varnish, suitable for paper. Ordinary oil varnishes must not be used as they will grease your work.

When dry, the brush will be a very attractive article and it will look worth a great deal more than sixpence or a shilling.

A MODERNISTIC DRAUGHT SCREEN

There are always many uses for a draught-screen in every house. The one we have illustrated here has the merit of being a little unusual in conception. First, the three sections are of different dimensions and, second, the pattern is of a modernistic character.

Each leaf is made of a frame of wooden strips, 1 inch square in section. The three are hinged together so that they will fold up flat. Canvas is pinned over the frame or, if the cost makes this material prohibitive, tough paper is used instead. The pattern is painted on after all the constructional work is finished. Poster colours are used when paper is the covering material, and dyes, such as are sold for tinting fabrics, when canvas is chosen.

Modernistic patterns are essentially broad in their arrangement and there is a total absence of niggling detail. Large masses broken by straight lines and circles, done in two or three colours, is what will serve best.

A DESK FOR YOUR DEN

Any boy who is capable of making good mortice joints can construct the desk, shown in the illustration, for about five shillings.

The wood is ordinary deal, stained or painted to resemble the other pieces of furniture that are to go with it.

All the necessary dimensions are shown.

The desk is made in two parts, (1) the base, and (2) the back case

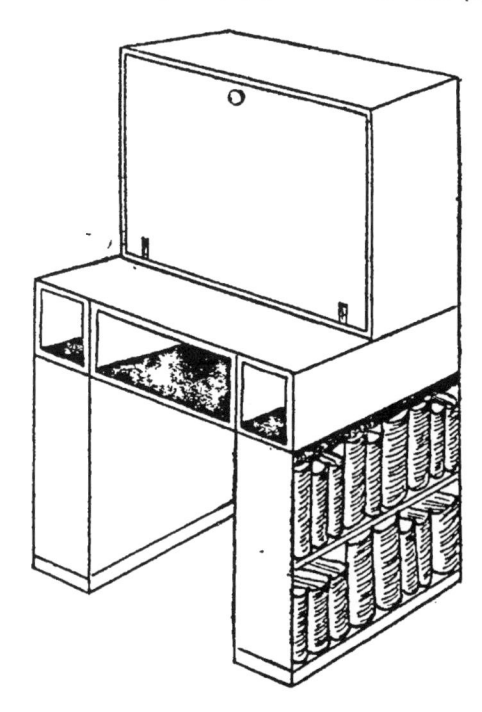

the hinged side of which swings downwards and makes a firm writing table. The two parts are held together by means of three stout screws which penetrate the floor of the back case and enter the base.

Inside the back case, there are two shelves, making three horizontal divisions. The two upper divisions take books, letters, boxes, etc., whilst the lower division is reserved for red and black ink-pots, a pen tray and sundry writing and drawing materials. The inner face of the lid, which serves as a writing table has sheets of blotting-paper pinned to it.

Above the knee-hole of the base are two or three compartments. In the ordinary way, these spaces are taken up by drawers ; but drawers are difficult to construct satisfactorily and are hardly worth attempting.

F

A better plan is to make the spaces and fill them, one each, with box files.

The two sides of the base are planned to take two rows of books each. This is an arrangement seldom provided with commercially-made desks; but it is a very attractive way of utilizing the space.

A STRONG WASTE-PAPER BASKET

A basket made of tinned iron is something of a contradiction, but that need not deter us in our work of making a very neat waste-paper basket out of a seven-pound biscuit tin.

Go to your grocer and get him to sell you a tin of this kind, if you do not already possess one. He will charge about tenpence. Then, soak the tin and scrape off all the paper labels. Be careful that you do not damage the thin metal by denting it, while doing this, because dents look very ugly and they are particularly difficult to flatten out. When all the paper has been removed and the tin is thoroughly dry, give it two or three coats of white enamel on the inside. You had better use a cellulose enamel because it dries very rapidly and so allows you to get on with the work more quickly.

The next step is to decide how you will ornament the outside of the tin. Here are some suggestions:

(1) Give two coats of black, then stencil a design on the four sides.

(2) Paint the sides in vertical stripes of various colours to obtain a jazz effect.

(3) Paint the sides white; then, dab a multitude of colours evenly over all the white to obtain a pleasing mottled effect.

(4) Paint the sides a brilliant colour, each side different, then paste a piece of paper centrally on each side. Let the pieces be cut to represent a heart, a diamond, a club and a spade.

(5) Use no paint at all, but paste some very attractive wall-paper over the sides.

(6) Cover all the sides with irregularly shaped pieces of silver paper, bearing patterns. Then apply a coat of varnish.

A HANDY RACK

This handy rack has a dozen or more uses. It consists of a spiral coil, slightly stretched and pinned down at both ends by means of a nail.

Let us suppose you would like a rack for small tools, fitted to the wall, behind your work bench. Get a spiral coil, not too fierce, stretch it a little and nail it, horizontally, just where you want to place your tools. If it has a tendency to sag down, run a stout piece wire through

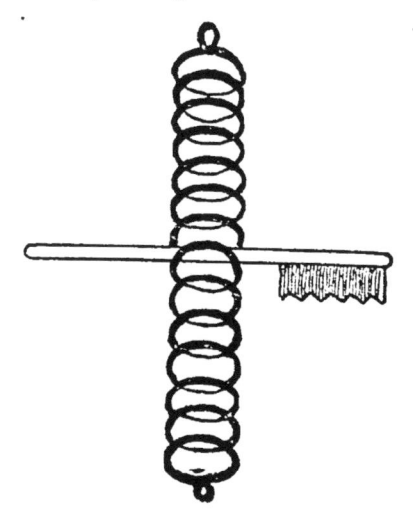

the coil, from end to end, and fix it to the wall, also. All sorts of small tools can now be held, with a vice-like grip, between any two consecutive loops of the wire. They can be pushed in or pulled out without the slightest trouble.

Place one of these racks on the bathroom wall and it will serve admirably for gripping tooth-brushes. The coil should be enamelled white, in this case.

MAKE YOUR OWN BOOKPLATE

A bookplate, inscribed with your name, adds a neat personal touch to the books which you possess. An extremely easy way to make a batch of these labels is as follows:—Take a sheet of fairly thin, tough paper, without an impressed watermark, and cut out of it a piece 3½ inches by 2½ inches. On this neatly print your name, your address if you wish, the words EX LIBRIS, and some suitable sketch by way of ornamentation. The sketch may well take the form of your school badge, or some device peculiar to the locality where you live. It is not a bad idea to add a few lines of poetry if you can think of anything suitable. Here is such a couplet often used:

"Wet or fine; rain or shine,
Kindly note this book is mine."

For all the printing and designing use indian rather than ordinary ink.

When the bookplate is finished, go to a photographic dealer and buy a printing frame to take pictures 3½ inches by 2½ inches; then get a packet of self-toning paper of the same size, and 1-lb. of hypo. On reaching home put a sheet of glass in the frame, then the design on thin paper, inked side to the glass; place on top of this a sheet of the self-toning paper, and print in the sun until the paper has become a dark brown. Then fix as directed by the instructions given in the packet. When dry, paste on to the cover of a book by means of photo-mountant. For half a crown you can make sufficient bookplates for an average boy's library.

A PAIR OF BOOK ENDS

Books which are lying about on your table give the room an untidy appearance ; in addition, they are sure to suffer damage. But, stand up the books in a row, put a heavy " book end," one at each end of the row, and neatness is, at once, secured.

You ought to make a pair of book ends. There are several ways of constructing them ; but for a boy's den, an elaborate decorative pattern is hardly suitable. You want a severely plain, yet attractive, pair.

Here is just the thing : a block of wood, 4 by 4 by 5 inches, and see that all the faces are perfectly smooth.

Next, cut two sheets of wood, 4 by 3 inches and ½ inch thick. Glue these to the block, one on each of the opposite " 5 by 4 inch " faces. Fit them exactly in the corners, a 4 inch side of the sheet running with a 5 inch side of the block.

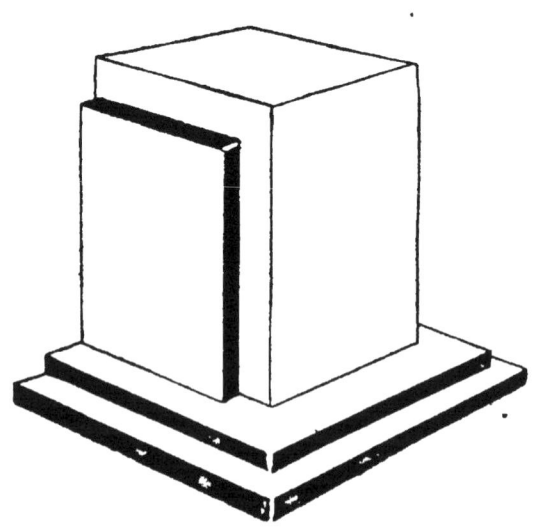

Now, cut a sheet of wood, 5 by 6 inches, and ½ inch thick, and glue one of the square faces of the block to it. The square face must be the one which has had the two thin sections brought to its edges. Place the block centrally on the sheet as far as three sides are concerned, but made the edges coincide on the fourth.

Follow this by cutting another sheet of wood, 6 by 7 inches and ½ inch thick, and glue it to the previous sheet. Here again, place the smaller sheet centrally on the larger sheet as far as three sides are concerned, but make the edges coincide on the fourth.

One book end is now constructed, and it will look like the diagram shown here. You will require a second one to complete the pair. Finally, colour the two, using vivid cellulose paints for the purpose. Do each face and ridge a different colour.

ANOTHER IDEA FOR BOOK ENDS

Here is another idea for a pair of book-ends. Take two books that are alike and for which you have no further interest. Let them be fairly substantial. Carefully remove all the pages and, in their place, glue a piece of wood which has exactly the same dimensions as the combined mass of pages. The covers will, thus, be stuck to the wood.

Before you glue the covers, however, obtain two pieces of sheet iron, each about 7 by 3 inches, and nail them to the wood as shown in the diagram. After that, you fix down the covers and, then, bend the projecting pieces of iron, at right-angles. The weight of the wood makes the books substantially heavy, and the right-angled strip of iron serves as a leg.

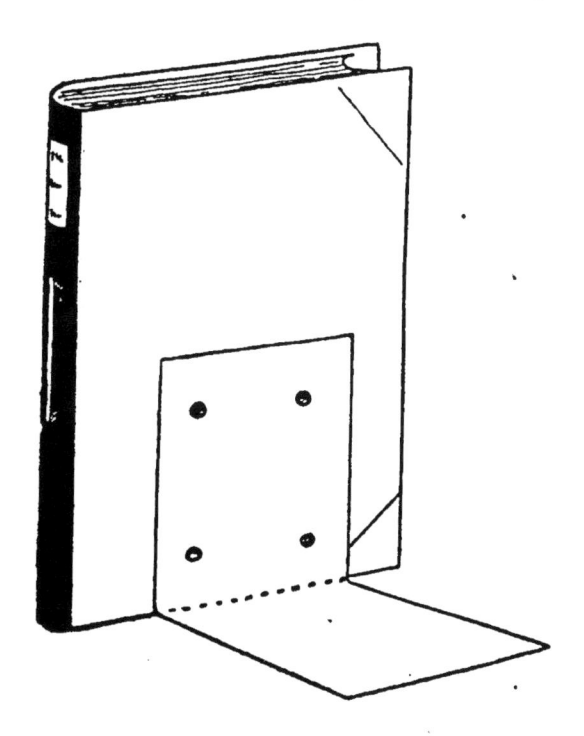

Note, particularly, that the two weighted books are to serve as a pair. Accordingly, one leg must be fixed to the front cover of one book, and the other leg to the back cover of the other book. One must turn one way and one the other, when fixed in position.

When the glue has set hard, paint the metal and disguise the edges of the wood so that they resemble a mass of pages. This can be done by using a dull red paint and drawing several pencil lines along it.

Of course, if you prefer, it is not a bad plan to give the entire books and the metal legs a coat of brilliant enamel paint.

It should be added that the book-ends ought to be stood with the legs projecting inwards, towards each other, so that books placed between stand on the projecting strips.

A RUBBER STAMP WITH YOUR INITIALS

A rubber stamp bearing your initials is useful for many purposes. You can make one, in the following way:

Cut a block of wood, 2 inches square and 1 inch thick—the exact dimensions are unimportant. Then obtain a small piece of bicycle tyre and cement it to the wood. Be careful that it lies flat and that there are no cockles.

When the cement has hardened, draw your initials, backwards, on the rubber, and cut away the portions which do not form the letters. If you find it difficult to imagine how the letters are shaped, backwards, draw them on a piece of paper and look at them in a mirror.

Of course, you can make stamps bearing patterns, geometrical designs, your school crest, and other things in exactly the same way.

A USEFUL COPYING APPARATUS

You probably have a hundred uses for a copying apparatus, one that will give from twenty to fifty impressions from a single copy. Though you cannot hope to possess a duplicating machine such as we see in use in city offices, the following little device will admirably serve your needs.

The requirements are :—(1) A flat tray, such as the lid of a biscuit tin, but it must be flat ; (2) 2 or 3 oz. of Scotch glue ; (3) about 8 oz. of glycerine ; and (4) a few drops of oil of cloves. Put the glue in a little warm water, and melt thoroughly ; then add the glycerine and oil of cloves. While still fluid pour into the tray and allow to set. It is best to melt the glue in a double saucepan—that is to say, in a small tin standing in a larger one containing hot water.

To make a number of duplicate copies, write the master copy on non-absorbent paper with hektograph ink. When the ink is quite dry, press on to the jelly surface, rub the back well, and after five minutes peel it off. Then apply blank sheets and rub well and peel off at once.

When all the required copies are taken, wash the surface of the jelly with a sponge and put it where it will not be damaged. When the surface becomes uneven by usage, melt slightly.

A HAT STAND

As you perhaps know, it spoils a lady's hat to hang it on a peg and, consequently, your mother and your sisters have to keep their hats on shelves and in similar places. Even when stored in this way, felts and other soft materials lose their proper shapes and much the best plan is to use a wooden stand, with the hat perched on the top.

From this, you will readily see that if you set to work and make two or three suitable stands, the feminine portion of your family will be considerably grateful. This is the way to make such a stand.

Obtain some wood, the section of which is 2 inches square. Cut off a length 15 inches long and fix to one end a square foot made of wood, 1 inch thick, and 5 by 5 inches. At the other end, screw on a top. This should be about 4 by 3 inches. Before fitting this last piece, cover the upper face rather loosely with a nice strip of cretonne or other attractive material. Fix it on the under face with small tacks; but leave one side open and, using this open edge, stuff the upper surface with soft pieces of rag. When you have made this pad nicely and regularly arched, tack up the remaining side.

If you think that the stand is not strong enough for its work, put an edging of wood around the base of the central stem, using two by two material for the purpose.

All the pieces should be smoothed carefully before the assembling is done, then the wood should be stained a dark brown. As an additional refinement, it is not a bad plan to stick a piece of green baize on the under face of the foot. Tube glue will do for the purpose.

You now have an excellent birthday present for your mother or sisters, or a suitable article to sell at a bazaar.

A FANCY TOWEL RACK

Small children are supposed to have a rooted dislike to washing themselves, and all sorts of things in the nature of inducements are offered them to make washing a more attractive business. Here is one that might be useful for your young brother.

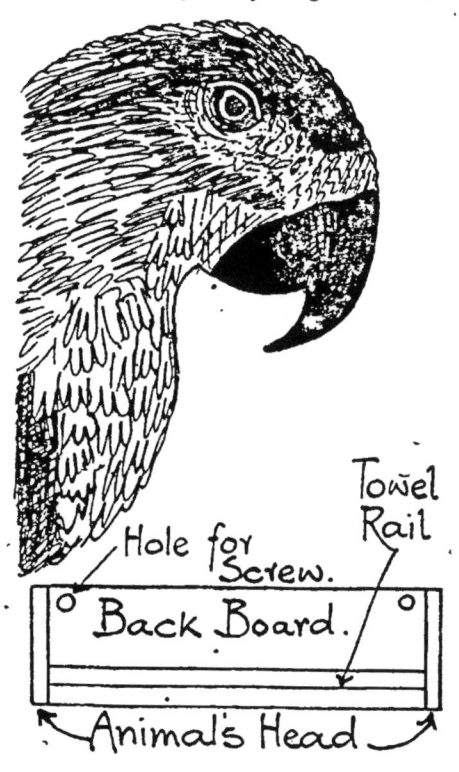

It consists of a fancy rack, which you can screw to the nursery or bathroom wall, to take his own particular towel. The rack consists of four parts, (1) a flat board, about 5 inches wide and 18 inches long, (2) a white painted curtain rod, the exact length of the board, and (3) two end brackets which are alike in shape.

The difference between this and any other towel rack is that the end brackets are shaped to imitate some animal's head. Naturally, you can choose whatever creature you like for the purpose, but it is advisable to avoid anything of a fearsome nature, such as tigers and wolves. We recently made one of these brackets and selected a bird's head for the purpose. The vivid plumage gave us the opportunity of introducing plenty of colour, which is, in itself, an attraction.

Whatever head you choose, plan it out on paper; then, transfer the outline to two separate pieces of wood, 1 inch thick, and cut them with a fret-saw, both exactly alike. The wood is a trifle thick for fret-saws, so you must be careful with the blade.

These head-shaped brackets are screwed to the end of the back board or better still, dove-tailed to it, if this is a job which you can undertake. But, before the pieces are joined together, a hole is bored in corresponding places in both of the heads, to take the circular rail.

All the constructional parts being completed, you coat the wood with a white cellulose paint, and when this has dried, the head is suitably coloured with other cellulose paints.

The last thing is to bore two holes, one near each end of the back board and fix the rack to the wall or door by means of long screws or nails.

CURING AN ANIMAL'S SKIN

Every boy, at some time or other, has an animal's skin which he would like to cure. This is how to do the work. Take a board, and on it nail down tightly the stretched skin. Place the fur side next to the board, and run the nails through the ragged edges. Now plaster the skin side with powdered alum and leave for two days, preferably in the sun. At the end of this time slightly moisten the alum and rub it well into the skin, and leave for another two days. On the fourth day repeat the whole of the alum application with fresh powder. On the completion of the second application remove the alum and go over the skin with fine glass-paper, and finish with a piece of pumice stone. This removes the little threads of sinews and rough skin. The skin is now very dry and stiff. To make it supple, rub it well with glycerine, but note that this substance ruins the fur. Hang out in the sun for a time, and, having shaken it well, it should be ready for use.

MAKING THINGS IN FRETWORK

If you are looking for a pastime that affords unlimited enjoyment, and, at the same time, helps you to become a handy individual, fretwork is certainly the thing to take up. It has given countless hours of pleasure to a vast army of boys, and it will do as much for you.

Fortunately, the necessary outfit is neither large nor expensive, and there is no need to buy a number of tools until you know whether you like the hobby or not. The things you must have at the outset are: (1) a fretwork saw with a dozen spare blades, (2) a V-shaped cutting table provided with a clamp, (3) an archimedean drill, (4) a pennyworth of fine glass-paper, (5) a small triangular file, and (6) a supply of suitable wood. Five shillings judiciously spent will set you up comfortably.

The first thing that you need consider is the wood. Of course, you

Hundreds of Things a Boy Can Make

will want fairly thin material, say about ⅛ inch thick. Three-ply is the cheapest material, and it answers quite well, but it is liable to splinter on the under side of the cuts, and may break rather more saw blades than better woods. The better woods consist of sheet mahogany, sycamore, beech, etc. These can be bought at no great cost, but are really too good for experimental work.

Having obtained a supply of wood, the next thing is to find a design. Very soon, you will scheme out your own patterns, but at first it will be wisest to copy those made by experts. You will find all you want in this direction in the weekly paper known as *Hobbies*.

The design and the wood being decided upon, paste the former on to the latter, using as little moisture as possible. We make this suggestion because a copious layer of wet paste will make the thin wood cockle.

Anyway, when the pasting has been done, put a weight on the surface, to press it down flat. Above all things, wait for the paper to dry, for if you cut when it is wet, the saw will drag out large areas of the pattern.

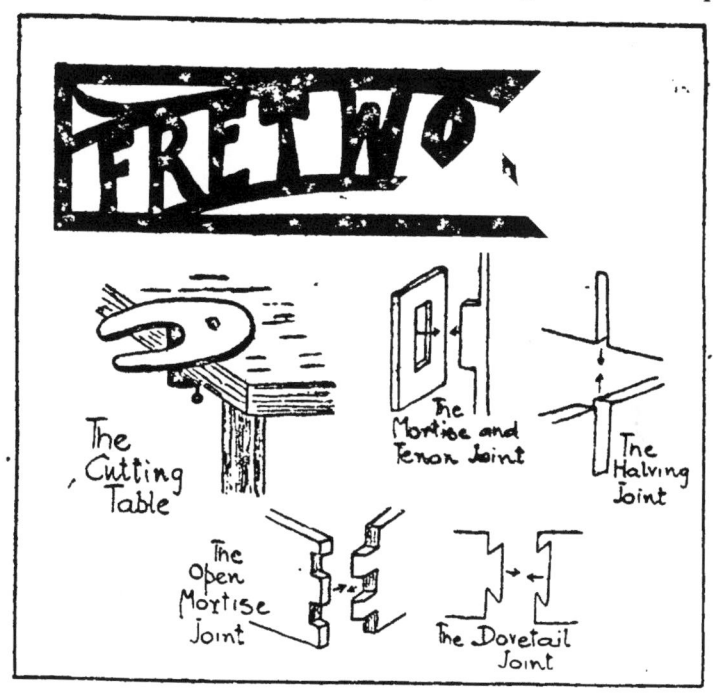

All being ready, note the parts that are to be cut out. Those that are "islands"—that is to say, those that are to be surrounded entirely by parts of the design—must be pierced. Do this with the archimedean drill.

Now to begin the actual work. Clamp the V-shaped cutting table—it is merely a firm disc of metal—on to the table in your den, lay the wood on top, undo the blade of the saw if it is fixed, pass it through one of the holes made by the drill, and refix into the saw handle. See that the blade is so arranged that the teeth cut by downward, and not by upward, strokes, and see, also, that the blade is just sufficiently tight. If too loose it will wobble, and if too firm it will snap.

In cutting, keep the saw erect, so that the new edges of the wood do not slant but are perfectly vertical. Many workers do not give sufficient attention to this part of the business, and not only do their designs look unfinished, but their joints are ill-fitting. It is more satisfactory to start in the middle of a design and proceed outwards, than to work in an opposite direction. This plan obviates some of the breaks and snaps that an inward course often occasions.

Having cut out all the various frets, the design is carefully examined and the fine file is brought into action. It will be useful for clearing away a jagged edge to a cut, and, still more useful, for shaping an angle that the saw cut imperfectly. When all these little points have been attended to, it will be well to get some of the glass-paper and rub up both faces of the wood. This will provide a nice finish; but do not scratch the surface by vigorous pressure.

Your first attempt should be an easy design, with as few circles, ovals, and repeated portions as possible. Repeated parts are hard, because the slightest difference in them is revealed at once. Later on, more difficult things will be attempted, which will include designs made up of more sections than one. You will then have to learn how to join the pieces. The most common joints are known as (1) the mortise and tenon, (2) the halving, (3) the open mortise, and (4) the dovetail joints, which are illustrated on page 89.

Each joint must fit exactly—the projection filling its corresponding depression with great accuracy. Any fault should err on the side of a tight rather than a loose fit, because more can always be pared away, but nothing can be replaced. When the fitting has been done, touch the edges with glue and press the parts together. The slightest application is sufficient.

An interesting part of the work consists in giving a finish to the wood, though this is not always necessary. A waxed or oiled surface suits many things; French polish looks best when done well, but staining is the most useful in the case of cheap woods, and it is a very simple process. Never fly to the cheap and nasty spirit varnishes. They look flashy at first, dingy later on, and are liable to chip as soon as dry and hard.

FRETWORK ARTICLES TO MAKE

Having read the previous article, you will now be able to make some of these things:

Hand Mirror.—This is a useful article and not difficult to make. Take the dimensions from an existing mirror in your home. Use mahogany and polish it. A piece of looking glass may be bought from the nearest glazier, whilst *Hobbies* sell a bevelled, oval mirror for one shilling and sixpence. Fix the mirror to the full shape by means of an overlay frame.

Clappers.—Two pairs of clappers, if you know how to use them, will make a great deal of rhythmical noise. Cut them out of scrap wood, 5 inches by 1½ inches, and bevel the edges.

Money Box.—Any wooden box with a good hinged lid and a small lock can be made into a money box. Stain it inside and out and put on each outer face a fretted design.

A Penholder Rack.—Cut a base board, 8 by 4 inches, and erect at each end a support for the penholders. The supports should have a series of cut-out half circles in which the penholders may rest.

Ink Stand and Penholder Rack.—As before, but slightly larger so that there is space for an inkpot in the centre of the baseboard. The pot fits in a raised collar, made of ornamental moulding.

Watch-Stand.—A panel, 6 by 3 inches, ornamented with a fretwork design. In the centre, a trifle below the upper edge, a small hook for taking the watch. A strutted leg, behind.

Toothbrush Rack.—A panel, 6 by 3 inches, ornamented with a fretwork design. Close to the lower edge is a horizontal shelf, perforated with two holes, each large enough to take the handle of a toothbrush. Paint the whole, with three coats of white " porcelainit," or similar paint.

Thermometer Stand.—A long, narrow panel of ornamental fretwork, 8 by 3 inches, with two brass clips for holding the thermometer, which can be bought for about a shilling.

Notepaper Rack.—The wood required is (*a*) a base, 9 by 4 inches, (*b*) a back, 9 by 6 inches, (*c*) a middle partition, 9 by 5 inches, (*d*) a front, 9 by 4 inches, (*e*) two sides, 6 by 4 inches but cut to a curved front. Join up with pins and glue. Provide frets in the upper portions of each of the upstanding sections.

Shaving Glass.—A square, ornamental foot, with 4 inch sides ; a pillar of wood $1\frac{1}{2}$ inches in section and 4 inches long, fitted to the centre of the foot. The mirror has a backing of wood, out of which stands a small wooden triangle. The triangle and the top of the pillar have a circular opening through which passes a nut and bolt, so that the mirror may be held at any angle. If top heavy, weight under the foot with sheet lead.

Toast Rack.—Three sections of wood, each 4 by 3 inches, ornamented with a fretwork design, and all jointed to a baseboard, 4 by 3 inches.

Glove Box.—Any nice wooden box, with a good lid, each side and the lid ornamented with a fret pattern.

Cigarette Box.—A box of such shape that a normal 3 inch cigarette will fit into it without more than a fraction of an inch to spare, treated as the glove box above.

Biscuit Box.—Make a wooden shell to fit around a tin of suitable size. Ornament the sides with fret designs and make a pull-off lid, with a convenient knob at top.

Medicine Chest.—A deal box, with lid made to fit against an internal flange, and provided with a catch. Inside, two compartments. Each outer side given a panel, done in fretwork. All painted with three coats of white enamel.

Crumb Tray.—A base of wood, 8 by 5 inches, with three raised edges, the remaining side being one of the long sides. The short edges must slope from back to front. Cut a fret pattern in them ; but only make a fairly large hole in centre of the longer side for handle. Plane the " mouth " edge of the base very narrow.

A Fireside Stool.—A deal box, about 12 by 10, by 6 inches. Nail lid down, add four ball feet. Stain a dark colour and cover the sides with an ornamental fret and the seat with a smooth piece of fret wood.

Umbrella Stand.—Four uprights, 2 foot 3 inches by 5 inches, fitted around a base of wood, 5 inches square. Each upright bearing a fret pattern. Two bands of polished brass fixed around the uprights, 18 inches apart. A metal tray made to fit in bottom of stand.

Jardinière.—A square deal box, large enough to take a good sized flower-pot. Four ball feet fitted and each of the four corners ornamented with a fret pattern.

Needlework Table.—A square deal box, with flap lid, carefully sand-papered. Four legs fitted to the corners, each 3 feet high and 1 inch square, in section. The four side panels and lid covered with a fret pattern. The inside lined with padded silk, if possible, or covered with leatherette paper.

Hanging Lamp.—Four sides each 6 by 4 inches. Each face, in turn has four rectangular cut-out spaces of similar size. A pyramidal roof made of thick cardboard, and having a small opening at top for support, above the electric light bulb. Glass inside, behind the barred openings. All painted black, both inside and out.

Hymn Board.—A back board, 2 feet by 1 foot, preferably made of light oak. At top and bottom, some overlay fretwork ornamentation. The word, "Hymns," should be placed at the top. Five equal spaces, made by fixing horizontal strips of moulding, to take the number cards.

Doll's House Furniture.—As a rule, these items are made of strip wood; but if cut by a fret-saw out of thin wood, it is possible to make them of fewer pieces and, consequently, they will be much stronger. A chair, for instance, should be made of three pieces only, i.e. (*a*) the back rest and back legs, (*b*) the two front legs and (*c*) the seat. Use glue for fixing, rather than pins.

Toy Shop.—Cut out pieces of thin wood to form a box-shaped enclosure, but leave out one of the larger faces. Pin and glue all the pieces together, and shape small fittings, such as a counter, a stack of shelves, etc., for displaying the stock of wares.

HE WAGS HIS TAIL

Here is an interesting model of a dog that wags his tail and nods his head. If you have a fret-saw, it is quite easy to make.

Note how it is put together. The head and tail are cut out of a single thickness of ordinary fret-wood. The body consists of two pieces, exactly alike in shape, but, within the dotted lines, there is a third piece, separating the two similar pieces. The dog is glued and pinned to a baseboard, through which there are two holes to enable the string to pass downwards.

In assembling the parts, it will be convenient to make up the body first. Put the internal section between the two similar pieces of the body and pin them together in four or five places. Then drill a hole from one surface to the other, to fix the head and the tail. Make a hole through the head and, also, through the tail, and fasten the three thicknesses, in each case, with a portion of a wire nail. Be careful to make all these holes sufficiently large to allow the wood to pivot freely round the nail and burr over the headless end of the nail, so that it will not slip out of position.

Before fixing the head and tail finally a hole should be bored through each, and a piece of string tied to the holes. The string is carried down

the body, as shown in the diagram, to the baseboard, which it passes through and continues for about the same distance as the length of the baseboard. The two pieces of string are, finally, tied together and fitted with a weight.

In action, the baseboard is clipped to the edge of a table, so that it overhangs, and then the weight is given a pendulum movement. As it sways to and fro, the head and tail rise and fall in a most amusing fashion.

THE CLIMBING MONKEY

Who wants a climbing monkey? Here is a capital little fellow you can make for two pence, and who will give you hours of fun. It is really a job for the boy with a fret-work outfit.

Get some very thin wood, stout cardboard will almost do, and cut out one piece shaped like A and two like B. Paint them up, anyhow you please, to look like a playful little monkey. Now fix two stout pins, as shown at C, in the thickness of the wood. Drive them in securely and as close together as you like. At D, drive in a long pin or piece of wire that does not bend too easily, and turn it round to form a loop. Next, take the piece of wood, A, and put the two pieces, B, one each side of it, and hinge the three thicknesses together by putting in a fastener at E. See that the three pieces " flop " about easily without coming undone. Before you do any more, get a thin elastic band, which is not quite as long as the distance, F to G. Bend a pin into a loop, clip off the head, thread one end of the elastic through the loop, and hammer the two ends into the thickness of the wood. Bring the elastic down to F, hold it there by means of another headless pin, and force each of the ends through the two pieces of wood, called B. The elastic band now pulls the legs up to the body, because the distance F to G was a little longer than the band itself.

There is not a great deal left to do, so let us proceed. Take a cheap pen-holder with a circular handle. Cut off two little bits, just a trifle thicker than the wood used for A, fit them between the two legs, B, at

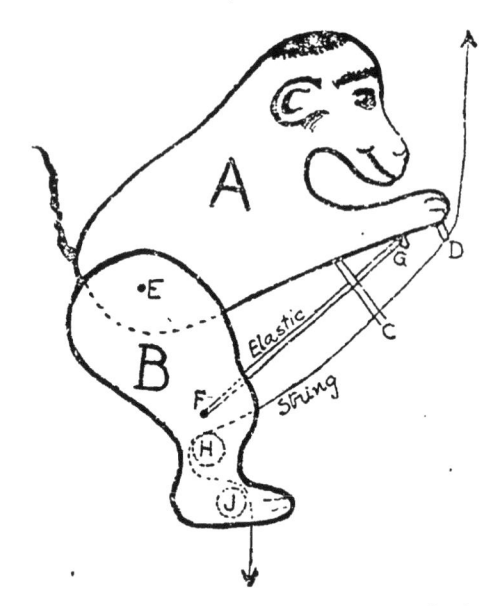

H and J by driving a pin through the wood and the pen-holder bits, and turning over the ends.

The last stage consists in taking a length of thin string about a yard long, threading it through D, then between the pins C, down behind the roller H and up in front of and over J. By the way, we forgot to say that the rubber band should pass outside the pins C, one strip each side.

Now, gently push the monkey down to nearly the bottom of the string, hold the ends of the string one in each hand in such a way that the string is vertical. Stretch up the top hand—and the body of the monkey moves upwards. Release some of the pressure of the lower hand, and the monkey's legs go up; repeat these actions a number of times, and his lordship climbs right up to the top of the string. It is the elastic that does the trick.

If you like, fix a little piece of twine on to the back to serve as a tail. That is all.

HARD LABOUR

This acrobatic gentleman can be made in various sizes. As a toy for a small child to pull along the floor, he will be best if cut out about 10 inches high. Should the figure be required for running up and down the table, 4 inches will be enough. Between these two extremes, you can make him according to whatever purpose you desire. Having determined his height, the vertical length of the frame should be the same and the horizontal length, about double.

The diagram almost explains the arrangement without the need for verbal description. The old gentleman is cut out of three-ply wood with the aid of a fret-saw. Paper is pasted to both sides, and his form is drawn and coloured on both. A round hole is, then, drilled through his body and a cylindrical piece of dowel rod is driven tightly through it.

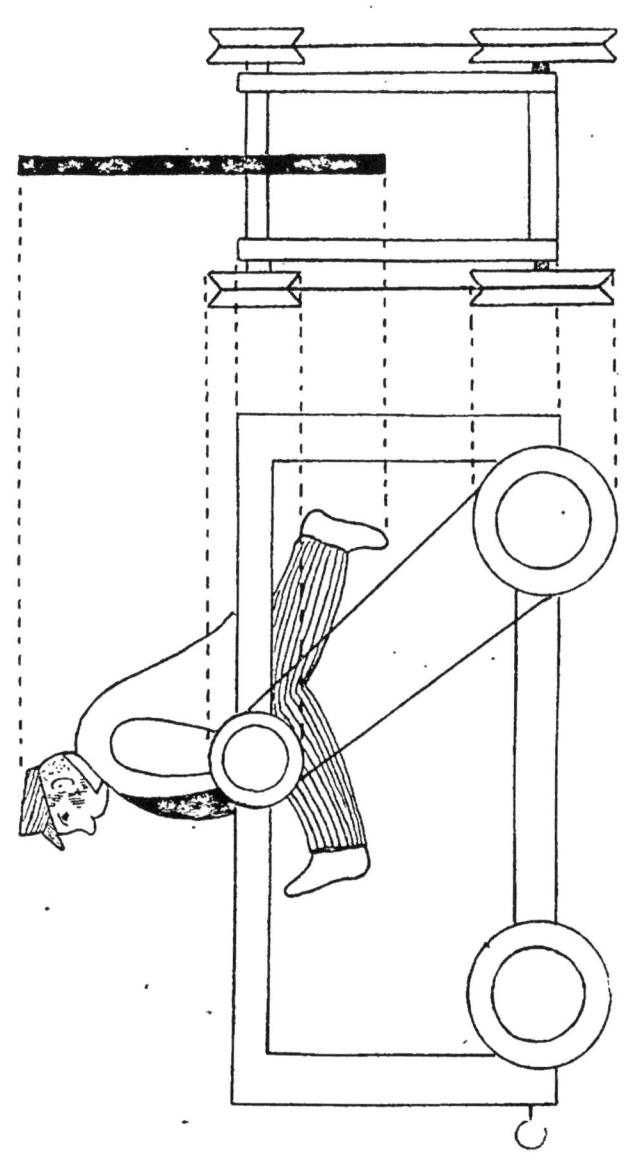

Next, cut out two frames from three-ply, exactly alike in size, and, in the centre of the upper edge of both, bore a hole to take the dowel rod; but, in this case, let the holes be large enough to allow the rod to turn freely within them.

Follow this by cutting a piece of wood, fairly stout in comparison with the other pieces, equal to the length of the frame and as wide as about half its height.

In assembling the parts, use this latter piece for the floor, then, nail the two frames to it along the bottom edge; but, before fixing the second frame, slip the gentleman and the dowel rod in the centre holes found in the upper edge of both frames.

The carriage part is now complete, and the wheels should be considered, at this point. Four large ones and two smaller ones are needed. Two of the former and both the latter must be provided with a groove in the tread, suitable for taking an elastic belt. If these wheels cannot be made or readily purchased, they may be obtained from the Meccano firm. The two upper wheels are wedged tightly to the ends of the dowel rod and the others will act efficiently if held to the carriage floor by means of a stout nail for each.

The fixing of the two belts needs no description.

The model is now finished. When it is drawn along, the supporting wheels revolve and the two rear wheels transmit their motion, by means of the belt fitted to each, to the wheels, one on each side of the dowel rod, which is made to revolve. As the dowel rod revolves, the old gentleman has to go with it and that is why he looks so distressed.

POLISHING THE WOODEN ARTICLES YOU CONSTRUCT

French polishing is not the mysterious art many people would have you believe. It is a fairly straightforward job, and as it provides so pleasing a finish, it is a process well worth acquiring. All you want, except the necessary patience, can be bought for a two shilling piece.

The ordinary polish can be bought from 1s. to 1s. 6d. per pint at most oil and colour stores, therefore it is hardly worth while making it yourself. It is necessary to have the work to be done in a warm, dry room, free from draught. The materials wanted are: polish, raw linseed oil, and spirits of wine; cotton wool, a piece of woollen cloth, and plenty of old, soft, clean rag, for the *polishing* part; but, before polishing, the work requires filling up. This is done either with *oil* or *size* stopping; for oil stopping all that is necessary is some boiled oil and whiting, made into a paste and stained to the colour wanted. This is to be well worked into the pores of the wood, by spreading over the surface with a piece of old coarse cloth, pressing it well at the same time. When the pores are well filled, rub over with an oil rag, and leave for a day; then rub to a good face with glass-paper and apply the polish.

If it is for a large surface, take a piece of woollen cloth about 2 or 3 inches wide, and 7 or 8 inches long, and roll it up to form a "pad." Cover this with two or three folds of clean soft rag, after having well wetted it with the polish; draw the ends of the rag into the palm of the hand to hold all firm, and with the fingers just touch the surface of the rag with a little linseed oil—this causes the polish to run through with greater freedom and prevents it from hardening too quickly.

Give three successive coats from end to end—that is, in the direction of the grain. After this, with a circular motion, go over it in a *cross* direction. Repeat this until a uniform and sufficient body of polish is transferred to the work; then let it stand a few hours until the spirit is absorbed and hard, after which lightly rub with fine glass-paper. Continue the process of polishing as before, until it looks as if a sheet of glass was laid upon it, and proceed to "finish," which is done with fresh rags; or, better still, some cotton wool with a few drops of spirits of wine applied on the surface, and lightly continue to rub until the rubbers become perfectly dry, when the polishing is complete.

Note.—(1) The lighter and quicker the movement, the better will be the finish. Do not allow the rubbers to "rest" on the work, or they will *partially dissolve* the polish and make it rough. At each application of the polish to the rag, a clean place must be found.

(2) To stop the work with size-stopping, some good plaster of Paris is mixed up with sufficient glue-size to bind it or make it fast, and whilst warm the work is covered with a sponge. When dry (which is much sooner than with the oil-stopping) sand-paper, dust, and proceed as above. Either of the above stoppings can be stained to any colour; the polish can also be stained. Bismarck brown probably provides the most useful colour.

TOY CALENDARS

What a fascinating number of toy calendars you can make for your friends if you possess a fret-saw! We give a specimen illustration to show the kind of thing that is easily constructed. You will want some wood a quarter of an inch thick and, in the present case, the length is

about 8 inches while the other dimensions are in proportion. The roof and the tiles may be drawn and coloured on paper, carefully cut out and then pasted to the wood. The black cat is preferably shaped out of black velvet, with white linen buttons for eyes and bristles for whiskers. The pages of the calendar should be neatly printed, using another calendar as a guide, and a dab of glue will hold them in position.

TABLE SKITTLES

For this you will want a square of wood 2 feet long, with an edging all round 2 inches high. At one corner, fix half a broom handle, standing with its base on the square. As it must be firm, it will be necessary to use substantial wood for the various parts. If you want to make the apparatus appear attractive, stain all the wood a deep oak and cover the square with green baize.

At the top of the broom handle fix a piece of good whipcord and at the other end of this cord tie a wooden ball. The length of the cord must be such that the ball should just *not* reach the edging around the board.

Next you will want nine skittles. These can be made by cutting pieces, each 6 inches long, from two or three additional broom handles and, by trimming them, making them slightly barrel-shaped. A rub up on glass-paper will provide a neat finish.

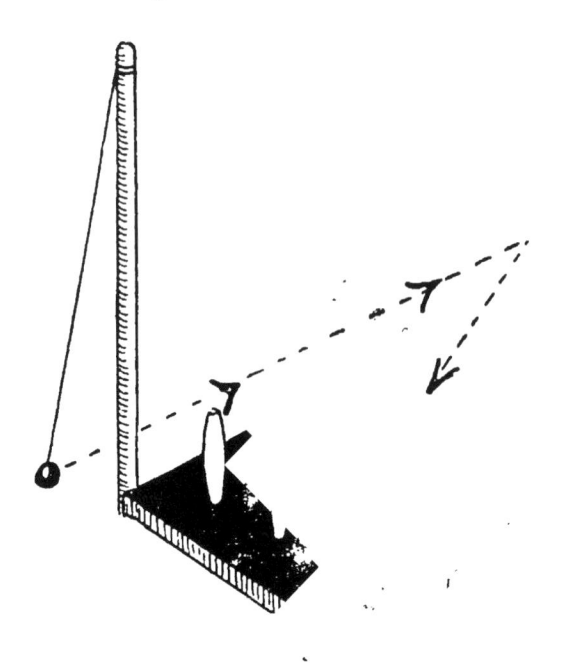

The table skittle-board is now finished. To use it, place the nine skittles as shown in the diagram, bring the ball attached to the string to the position shown in the diagram and let it go with a slight jerk. The ball must not hit the skittles by a direct shot, but must take the course shown by the arrows and the dotted lines. On the return it will probably knock over some of the skittles. The game is to capsize as many as possible—the whole nine, if you can.

AT YOUR SERVICE, MR. SMOKER

Have you seen those humorous figures which stand about three to four feet high and which conveniently hold out to you an ash tray? As a rule, they depict some grotesque individual, such as a leering page boy who is garbed in raiment of gaudy colours.

If you possess a fret-saw, you can make one of these quaint creatures fairly easily and he will prove very useful in the smoke-room or lounge.

First of all, get some wood, a quarter of an inch thick. You will want a strip about 3½ feet long and 1½ feet wide. Also, you will require a smaller piece, about a foot square. Three-ply will answer for the purpose, if you have mastered the knack of sawing it without breaking blades.

Place the larger piece of wood flat on a table and, with a pencil, mark the outline of your chosen figure. We have drawn what we think is a suitable character for the purpose, but you may prefer to originate your own individual.

When the outline has been done satisfactorily in pencil, cut it out with the fret-saw and, afterwards, trim up the smaller piece of wood to

serve as a foot. For this, a heart, diamond, club or spade is generally selected.

You will, now, have to shape up a piece of wood to place in the fellow's hand. It is really a ledge or shelf on which to stand the ash-tray. This shape can, usually, be trimmed out of some of the waste left over when the figure was made. A rectangular shape is as good as any for this.

The next step will be to fit the three pieces together. Much the best plan will be to dove-tail or mortise the feet to the base and the tray to the body. You must do this accurately, but it will not be a difficult job if you pencil the places that have to be cut, and use a sharp chisel for making the holes. When the cutting is finished, the pieces should fit together tightly; but they should be given extra strength by means of glue, whilst under the tray, a small bracket should be screwed.

If you do not care to attempt dove-tailing, almost as good results may be obtained by nailing narrow strips of wood in the angles made where the wood is joined.

The constructional part is now finished and the colouring remains to be taken in hand. Use bright cellulose colours. They will dry quickly and allow you to proceed more rapidly with the work than will ordinary oil paints. Moreover, they will present a more brilliant appearance.

As soon as the figure is dry, it is ready for use as a handy ash-tray.

Of course, you can add to the construction in various ways. In the case of the character shown in the illustration, it will be necessary to shape his grotesque shoes out of some suitable material. It would not be a bad plan to ram an old pair of gym shoes, full of paper, and to cover them with white calico.

BEAUTIFUL SMOKE RINGS

Some people can make smoke rings by filling their mouths with the smoke of a cigarette and jerking it into the air. You can easily make a little piece of apparatus which does the work far better than the mouth and in a much more scientific way.

Obtain a tin as large as possible and having each side approximately a square. If you cannot find such a tin it ought not to be difficult to make one out of a sheet of zinc and a little solder.

At the end opposite the lid cut a round hole in the centre. It can be done with a tin-opener, and it ought to be about $2\frac{1}{2}$ inches in diameter. Instead of the lid fix a piece of calico as tight as a drum and glue down the overlapping edges.

Now take a small bundle of rags, push it into the middle of the tin by way of the opening, and light it with a taper. The rags will not burst into flame but will smoulder. Put your hand over the round opening, so that the smoke will be retained in the tin. When it is fairly well charged take away your hand and give a series of jerky taps on the face of calico. Each tap expels a puff of smoke from the box, and it will be in the shape of a beautiful ring.

MAKING AN INTERESTING STAMP COLLECTION

A stamp collection can be a very dreary possession if it consists of rows and rows of stamps and nothing more. True, the bright colours and the attractive designs may please the eye, but, if this is all that is sought after, one might as well amass little bits of cretonne, labels from jam pots, or anything else that shows colouring.

Enlightened collectors no longer marshal their stamps in meaningless rows. They take the view that if a stamp is worth collecting, its history and all about it is worth knowing. In order to explain this view, let us suppose that we are dealing with the issues of Bermuda, then this is how they would be set out :

On a blank page of a loose-leaf album, the word " Bermuda " would be printed first. Then would come the following information : " Bermuda is a British possession. It consists of about 360 small islands in the North Atlantic Ocean, 600 miles S.E. of Cape Hatteras. The natives are mostly black. Population, 22,000." If possible, a neat sketch map would be added to show exactly where the islands lie.

After this brief introduction, the stamps themselves would be set out; but they would not be left to state their own case. This would be done for them. Each set would be introduced with the date of issue, where printed, why the set was issued, and so on. One set, for instance, commemorates the "Tercentenary of the Establishment of Representative Institutions." This fact would be mentioned and its meaning explained.

From this it will be seen that an enormous amount of history and geography can be gleaned from an up-to-date collection. But these are not the only subjects which are made interesting by the proper treatment of a collection. There are a dozen others, all equally fascinating.

Accordingly, we advise you to scrap the old kind of album, to use a loose-leaf book, and to write every noteworthy fact in the book which you can discover about your stamps. The collection will then be full of interest, and you will never grow weary of turning over its pages and admiring your acquisitions.

Everybody's Pocket Gazetteer, a shilling Foulsham publication, will help you with the matter introducing each country, while an ordinary stamp catalogue provides the rest of the necessary information.

PRINTING A POSTER

It is very useful to be able to print, for notices of various kinds are constantly required at school, at the Scouts' quarters, at your club, and elsewhere. If you can be depended upon for producing, say, a well-lettered poster, you will become very popular.

The great thing in printing is to know how to form the letters. "That's quite simple," you may say : but try it. Before you have gone very far, as likely as not you will be wondering how this or that letter should be shaped or spaced in relation to the letter that has gone before. You will soon realise that it is not so easy as it seems.

If you want to excel at printing, your best plan is to hunt through the advertisements in newspapers and magazines, and to cut out any word that seems attractive to you. All such cuttings should be pasted into a book, and, when you have a few moments to spare, it will be a good plan to copy them on a sheet of rough paper, doing them sometimes the actual size, sometimes large enough for poster work. Very soon, you will gain a facility for printing that will stand you in good stead.

For poster-lettering, you cannot do better than procure a number of small bottles of different-coloured inks. By their aid, your work will be smart and attractive. Note, however, that when a poster is to be displayed in the open, where rain may beat on it, the only thing to use is fixed Indian ink. If the letters are to be large, a fine brush will be more serviceable than a pen-nib.

" COUNTING OUT "

Draw this figure, then try to work out the puzzle with or without the aid of your friends.

What you have to do is to select any number you like, say 19, then start at one and count round the spaces until you have counted nineteen, going in the direction of the arrow. The nineteenth space will be number six. So you draw a pencil line through number six, and leave it out of all subsequent counts.

You begin again, and as you left off at six, you start at seven and count nineteen. This will take you to number thirteen, since six has disappeared.

You begin once again, and, as you left off at thirteen, a recommencement is made at one. Now, six and thirteen are gone, so counting up to nineteen brings you to nine, which you cross out.

You proceed in this way, and the game is to select nineteen or any other number, so that the black one is the last remaining section, all the others having been crossed out.

When you have discovered a number that answers, make another circle with a different amount of spaces. Perhaps, you would like to know that twenty-one is the number that serves with our figure.

YOUR OWN CINEMA

This is a good idea. Take an old magazine that nobody wants and draw little pictures in the top right-hand corner of the odd-numbered pages. If the pictures are made to "follow on," that is to say, each one represents a movement of the same individual or thing, and if the pages are spun through with the thumb of the left hand, then an admirable movie picture will be the result.

The pictures will, of course, be small because the white margin space of each page is small, but that does not detract from the "film."

In constructing the "reel," try to get each picture exactly over the preceding one, and begin at the last page and work towards the first page. Do not attempt anything elaborate as there must be at least fifty different pictures, and unnecessary time spent on one will have to be repeated in the other forty-nine cases.

Hundreds of Things a Boy Can Make 103

Try something of the following kind : (1) a face ; (2) mouth opens ;
(3) tongue comes out ; (4) tongue goes in ; (5) mouth shuts ; (6) eyes

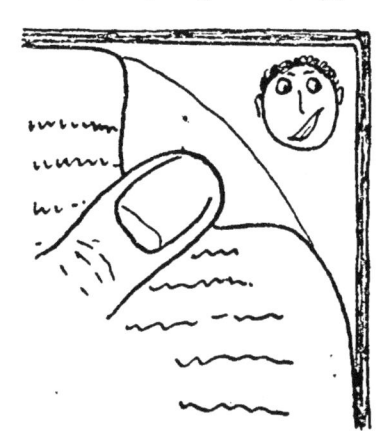

roll ; (7) face smiles, etc. This will be quite easy to draw and a good deal of fun may be obtained by changing the facial expressions.

WHAT DOES YOUR VOICE LOOK LIKE ?

That seems a silly question to ask. Nevertheless, we ask you, " What does your voice look like ? " You have never seen it, you reply. Well, this is how it can be seen. Take a round tin without a lid—we have used a toffee tin for the purpose. Then make a circular hole in it, about half way down the side. Into this, fit a piece of rubber piping. Have it a foot long, and insert a glass funnel into the free end. All the joins must be tight and well made. Now, over the top of the tin, tie a piece of parchment paper, such as your mother uses for covering jam-jars. Fit the paper as she does—that is, make it wet first. When dry, it will be as tight as a drum. On to the surface sprinkle some fine and dry silver sand.

The " Voice Illustrator " is now ready. Place the funnel to your lips and sound one good, full note. The sand will jump about and assume a symmetrical pattern. It is the picture of your voice. Note that as you leave off, there is a tendency for the pattern to break up and become spoiled. To prevent this, continue to sound the note, but draw the lips away from the funnel. You can then look at your voice as long as you like.

Before the next person makes his pictorial sound, give the tin a shake, and spread on more sand if any has been spilt.

Wonderful, isn't it, that everybody's voice makes a different picture.

A TIVOLI BOARD

In case you do not know exactly what a Tivoli board is, we have provided a sketch of one. It consists of a flat base, a little more than twice as long as wide, with an edging all round. At one end are several compartments, usually about six. All bear a number except one and this contains a spring rod. The other end is given a curved edging. Dotted about on the main part of the board are countless upstanding nails or pins. Play consists in putting a marble in the compartment provided with the spring rod, pulling the rod and driving the marble up the board. It hits the curved edging, rebounds, and threads its way back to the numbered compartments. Whichever one it enters counts as many points to the player as are marked on it.

For the base of the board, a piece of wood a quarter of an inch thick will be suitable. Let it be about 18 inches long and 10 inches wide. Make the edging of the same material. It should stand up about an inch

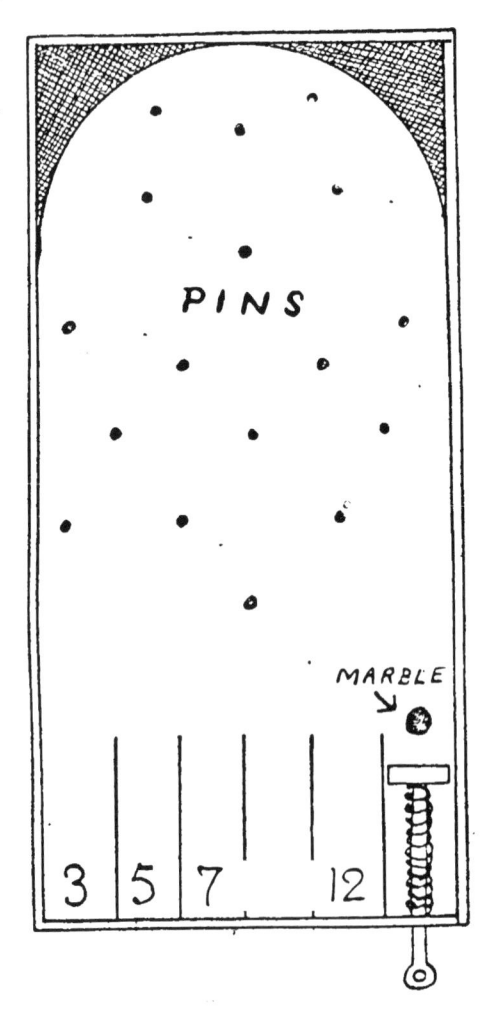

and a half. Use small panel pins for joining the sections together. The curved wall is most conveniently constructed from a piece of stout cardboard which should be shaved quite thin at the ends so that it does not project out in the area of play. Glue will fix it in position. The several compartments are provided by using similar wood to the base and gluing the pieces.

The spring rod is made of dowelling, a quarter of an inch thick and 4 inches long. At one end of it is placed a metal or wooden knob and at the other end a piece of wood, not quite as wide as the compartment into which it fits. Before these two terminals are fitted a spiral spring, which can be bought for twopence, is slipped round the dowel rod, and the end of the rod itself is passed through the edge of the board. It is clear, then, that when the rod is pulled a considerable way through the hole and out of the board, the spring coil is much constricted and, when the rod is let go, the coil bounds forward and takes the rod forward with it. This causes the flat tip of the rod to hit the marble and jerk it into play.

A PIPE RACK

A pipe rack is always a handy thing to hang on the wall, where smokers are concerned. Moreover, it serves as a capital Christmas or birthday present, and it has the additional merit of being very easy to construct.

You will want a piece of wood, about 8 inches by 4 inches and ½ inch thick. Square this up carefully and bevel the face edges with sandpaper. Then, obtain a strip of sheet brass, half an inch wide, and bend it, as shown in the diagram. This piece of metal is screwed on to the rack, and then it serves to carry the pipes.

Before you fix the strip of metal, decide how you will ornament the board, but make up your mind exactly where the metal strip is to be arranged. Not a bad idea is to do a poker-work design on the wood. You need not buy all the proper tools for this form of ornamentation. Two bradawls, heated in turn, can be used very successfully for the purpose.

A HOME-MADE MAGNIFYING GLASS

It often happens that a piece of useful apparatus which costs a great deal of money to buy, can be made out of odds and ends of material at practically no cost at all. For a magnifying glass, for instance, you may have to pay considerably more than a week's pocket money, yet here is a way to construct a make-shift magnifier for nothing.

Take a strip of grease-proof paper, half an inch wide and roll it in a band round an ordinary pencil. Let it encircle the pencil twice ; then touch the loose end with a drop of glue and stick it down.

When the glue has hardened, slip the band off the pencil, as carefully as you can, and stand the little tube, end on, on a sheet of clean glass. Support the glass on two boxes, so that it is 4 or 5 inches above the table and it must be quite level.

Next, take a fountain-pen filler and carefully fill the paper tube with water. Do this drop by drop, and, when you reach the top, put in the water so that the surface is convex. You are able to manage this owing to the property which water possesses, known as " surface-tension."

106   Hundreds of Things a Boy Can Make

Your magnifying glass is complete. On another sheet of glass, place the object which you want to see enlarged and slip it under the tube of water. By getting the distance just right, you will be able to view the object on a much larger scale than it really is.

MAGIC INKS

Here are some inks with which you may play tricks on your friends.

Make a weak solution of nitrate of copper. Write with it, using a clean nib, and leave to dry. When you wish to surprise your friends, hold the plain paper before the fire and the lettering comes into view, being red in colour.

Again, take a solution of tincture of iron. Make it just strong enough to write invisible characters. The words will become readable if the sheet of paper is pressed between blotting paper that has been dipped in strong tea.

An ink that vanishes on its own account is also useful at times. Here is a recipe for the purpose. Get some nut-galls and heat them in alcohol, but be careful of fire. Then mix with the alcohol some sal ammoniac and copper sulphate, and when quite cold add a spoonful of ordinary gum. Words written with this ink disappear in about a day.

CAN YOU SEE THROUGH A BRICK ?

This is one of those apparently impossible things that becomes possible with a little ingenuity. Look at the first diagram. There you see a little piece of apparatus, easily made, which will enable you to look right through the heaviest brick you can find.

First, get your brick and build the apparatus round it. Three-ply wood is the best material to use for making the contrivance, but we have constructed quite a rigid affair out of odd pieces of Beaver board, which is a form of tough cardboard.

The contrivance is a kind of enclosed arch, which goes round the brick. It must be shut in everywhere except at A and B, which are round openings through which to look. Inside, four slanting mirrors are fitted, as shown in the second diagram. Glass mirrors serve best for this purpose, but glass is a trifle heavy; we used highly polished sheet iron and found it answered admirably. Of course, the mirror must be as wide as the tunnel.

Use the contrivance as follows. Ask your friends whether they can see through a brick. On getting a rather superior " No " for answer, suggest that the thing is not impossible. Tell them to hold one of their hands at B, and then look through the hole at A, while the brick C bars the line of vision. The impossible becomes possible, thanks to your little piece of apparatus.

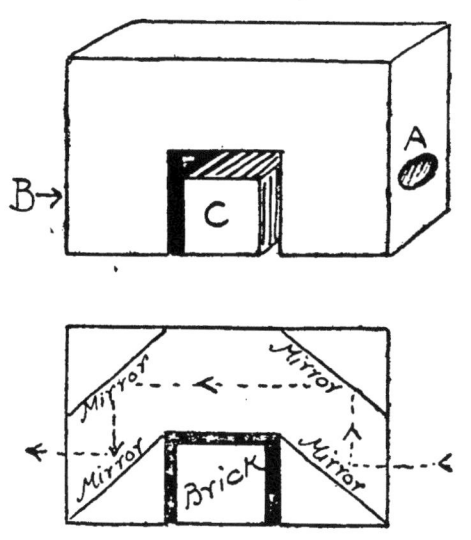

AN IDEA FOR JIGSAW PUZZLES

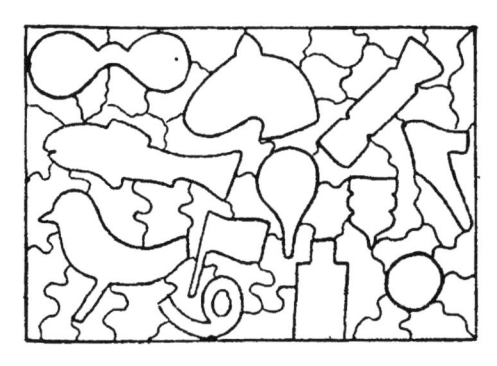

Of course, you will occasionally make jigsaw puzzles if you possess a fretwork outfit. Next time you set out to cut one, do it on these novel lines. Paste the picture on to the thin wood, then turn it over and draw, in pencil, on the back all sorts of attractive shapes, such as that of a fish, a horse's head, a peg-top, Cinderella's slipper, a Christmas cracker, a kite, a pair of specs, and so on. Then when you cut the puzzle follow the outline of these shapes. The pieces will be far more interesting than the ordinary odd sections, and when your friends make up the puzzles they will find the task much more enjoyable. Of course you will have to cut the pieces coming between the shapes in the usual manner.

MAKING PAPIER-MÂCHÉ MODELS

Model-making is a very popular pastime with boys. Some make replicas of well-known aeroplanes, others construct miniature Miss Englands ; others, again, find pleasure in building up rolling stock for their railway track.

When making these and many similar things, the difficulty, always, is to select a suitable material for the purpose. Although thin wood and sheet metal are excellent in their own particular way, there is another material that possesses many real advantages. It is papier-maché.

Papier-maché is easily made, it is remarkably strong, it can be waterproofed, it may be rubbed up with glass-paper and given a neat finish, and it is very cheap. It has one or two drawbacks, it is true, but they will be explained later.

Let us suppose that you wish to construct the hull of a boat. Sheet metal will hardly serve for the purpose, unless great pains are taken, and wood will be difficult to shape nicely. Papier-maché, on the other hand, will prove to be just the thing. First, it will be necessary to make the inside shape of the hull of cardboard. This part of the work can be done roughly and need take no more than a few minutes.

Next, you will want some paste. Take about half a pound of starch, mix it into a cream with a little cold water ; then add sufficient boiling water to make a pint of paste. Mind that the water is actually boiling, when used. If it has gone off the boil, it will not provide a paste that has proper adhesive qualities.

After that, tear up some sheets of newspaper into rough strips, approximately 1 by 2 inches.

When all is ready, paint the cardboard with a generous covering of the paste and stick on the strips of paper. Put them on without any idea of regularity, but aim at producing a final shape that approximates the shape desired. As each strip goes on, coat it all over with paste, and, with the brush, force it well into contact with the underneath strips.

When the desired shape has been obtained, the paper will not appear very attractive ; in fact, it will seem to be a most messy affair. But, never mind ; put the hull on one side and leave it to dry for several days.

After a time, the paper will become remarkably hard and tough. The cardboard interior may shrink away from the papier-maché, or, if it does not, the two materials are easily separated by running a table knife between them.

You now have a very strong hull for your boat, but it will be roughly shaped. Therefore, take some fine glass-paper and gradually give the model the lines and curves you require. This is not difficult ; in fact, it is surprising how easy it will be to impart to the hull whatever shape is desired.

When the shape has been perfected, the papier-maché may be painted with oils, it may be varnished, coated with shellac, or given almost any of the usual finishes.

Hundreds of Things a Boy Can Make 109

The drawbacks to papier-mache, as a modelling medium, are (1) it takes several days to dry and harden, and (2) it is not easy to make enclosed models with it.

CUT-OUT DESIGNS

A good deal of fun can be obtained with a pair of scissors and a sheet of paper. When next you have two or three of your boy friends round at your house, provide them each with scissors and a square of paper, and challenge them to make the best design with the least number of cuts. A sheet three inches each way will do nicely, and if possible, select

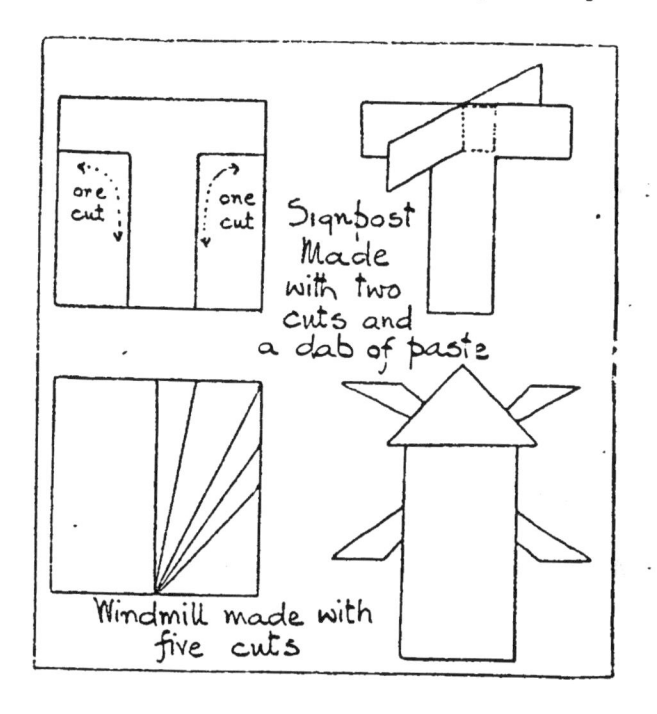

[Illustration: one cut / one cut — Signpost Made with two cuts and a dab of paste — Windmill made with five cuts]

paper that is covered with squares. Provide a pot of paste, in case one of the competitors wishes to stick part of his design, though you should make it clear that a design assembled flat on the table will be quite in order. We give here two specimen designs by way of examples. Note that in the case of the signpost, there are two right-angled cuts. The pieces cut out are slightly bent, as suggested by the dotted lines, and pasted on to the upper horizontal arm.

A "T" PUZZLE

Get some stiff paper and draw the letter "T" so that the width at any part measures one inch; and when you have done this cut it out neatly.

Next divide it up into four sections; but do it very carefully. First see that the cut marked B meets the cut A somewhere close to its middle point, not at its end. And try to make the lowest piece of the vertical leg almost but not quite equal in length to the section of the arm, at the right. Note, also, that the cuts A and C should not be parallel.

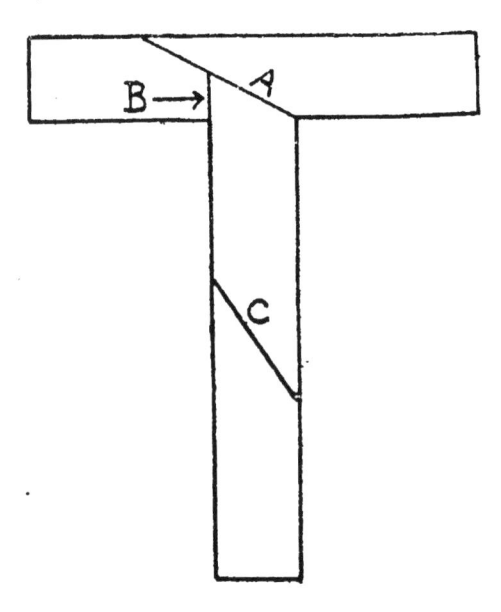

If you follow these instructions you will have a very easy-looking puzzle which will be really difficult to solve.

Try it on your friends. Shuffle the four pieces and ask them to re-form the letter T.

THE PAPER SHAPE OF FIVE SQUARES

This is a good puzzle that will exercise your ingenuity. Draw six equal squares on a piece of stout paper, placing them in three rows of twos. Then cut them out in one piece, but omit to include the uppermost left-hand square. The shape will be like that shown in Diagram A.

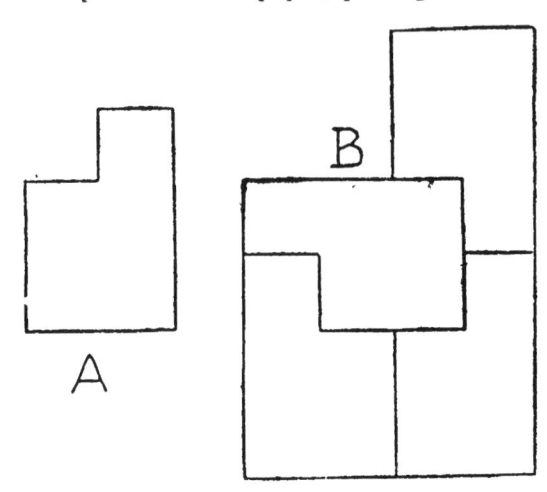

It is not a very attractive-looking piece of paper, it is true, but that hardly matters. Now what you have to do is to cut out three more of them, making four in all.

The puzzle consists in taking the four pieces and placing them together, so that the new figure, so formed, is the same shape as each piece, but considerably larger.

Diagram B shows how to do it.

WHAT A CLATTER !

This noisy toy can be made in a few moments. Cut out two pieces of cardboard, exactly the same size, shaped like the bat used in playing ping-pong or table-tennis. It should not be quite so large, however. Then measure its full length from tip to handle and obtain a strip of wood the same length. The wood should be about three-eighths of an inch wide and about a quarter of an inch thick.

Place the two pieces of card exactly one over the other, with the strip of wood running between them. Glue the two cards to the wood along no more than the end half of the handle, and, if possible, drive two nails through to add strength to the join.

Wait patiently until the glue has dried hard, then grip the handle and shake the little contrivance. Everybody will remark, " What a clatter ! "

The diagram shows the clapper with one flap removed.

ALL IN A ROW

Here is something that will help to give you a great deal of pleasure on a winter's evening. Obtain four ordinary post cards and cut out of them twenty-four circles, each about the size of a penny. If they are a trifle larger it will not matter ; but it is advisable not to have them smaller. See that all the discs will lie flat.

Now select two small players, give each of them twelve of the imitation pennies, and stand them one each side of the dining-room table. It is the longer sides of the table that we mean.

The players hold the pile of pennies in their hands and at the word

"Go," they put the pennies in line along their own edge of the table. They must begin right at the corner, and there must be no spaces between the coins. When the twelve are used up, the first to be laid is lifted and placed beside the last one, and so on, until the far corner of the table is reached. The player to reach it first is the winner.

MAKING A COLLECTING-BOX

Many boys are active members of church societies and other bodies which periodically make public appeals for funds. To be able to construct collecting boxes is, then, very helpful.

Here, we give some useful hints on how to make a substantial wooden box for the purpose. If less permanent boxes are preferred, it will be perfectly simple to substitute cheaper materials, such as cardboard, for those mentioned.

The requirements for each box are:

(1) Two pieces of wood, each 6 inches square and a quarter of an inch thick.
(2) Two pieces, 12 by 6 inches, of the same substance.
(3) One piece, 12 by 5½ inches.
(4) Two strips, 12 by 3 inches.
(5) A supply of 1 inch panel pins.

Having obtained the materials, place piece No. 3 on the bench and let it serve as the bottom of the box. Then, take the two pieces, listed as No. 2, and place them upright on the bench, in contact with the long edges of the bottom piece. Nail them in position with a few panel pins. Use these pins instead of ordinary nails as they are less likely to split the wood.

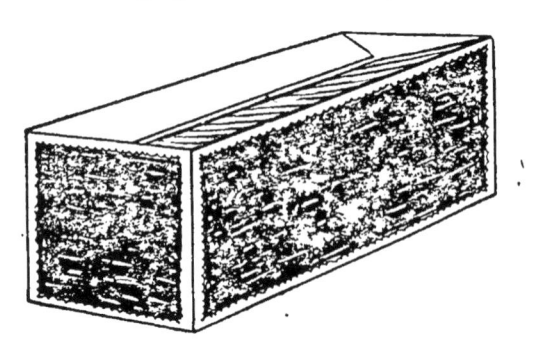

This done, take the two pieces, mentioned as No. 1, and fix them so that they serve as the ends to the box. If at this point, any piece of wood stands up longer than it should, use the spoke-shave to make it even with the other pieces.

So far, there is no top to the box. As will be seen from the diagram, this is to be composed of two strips of wood, which slope downwards towards the centre, with a slot about an eighth of an inch wide in the middle.

To fix these pieces, listed as No. 4, decide on the slope that will bring them to within about an eighth of an inch of each other and mark the lines on the inner face of the end pieces. Immediately below the pencil lines, drive in a few pins and rest the wood on them. This will help to keep the strips in position while they are being fixed. Afterwards, draw out the first set of pins, as they serve no further purpose.

Do not forget that some method must be devised for emptying the coins out of the box. The usual plan is to cut out a small section, along the bottom edge of one of the sides, before the fitting is done. Over this a sheet of paper is pasted and it must bear the signature or the stamp of the collector's authority. Naturally, the sheet is renewed each time the box is emptied.

There are countless ways of decorating such a box—paint, poker-work, carving and metal-inlay are a few suggestions which may be considered when an ornamental effect is desired.

TINTING ELECTRIC LIGHT BULBS

For parties and other festive occasions, a few tinted electric light bulbs produce a very happy effect.

Colouring ordinary bulbs is easily done in the following way. Buy a tin of water-glass, such as is used for pickling eggs, then obtain two or three packets of aniline dyes, of different colours.

Take small quantities of the water-glass and tint them differently; then pour the liquid on the bulbs and brush over the surfaces. Do **not** make the mistake of colouring the water-glass too strongly. Light shades are the most brilliant. Remember that by mixing small quantities of two different dyes, secondary colours can be produced.

PERPETUAL MOTION—ALMOST

The diagram suggests a rather weird looking wheel; nevertheless, it is an interesting little thing to construct. There is a centre cork, which is made by cutting—in halves—a cork out of a wine bottle. Next there

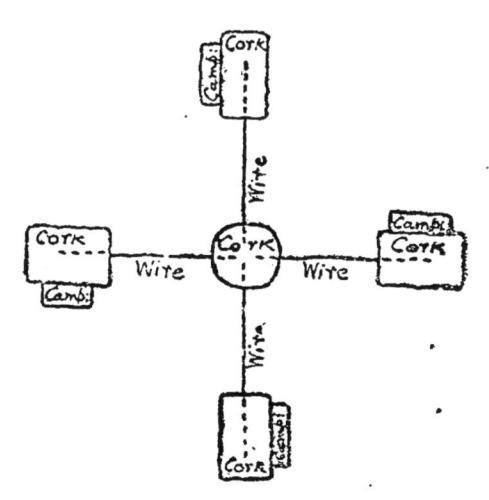

are four pieces of wire of equal length and weight. They are fixed, spoke fashion, into the central piece of arm. The outside ends of the wire are driven into four more pieces of cork, which should be, for preference, rectangular; but corks from wine bottles, vertically halved, will do as a makeshift. On to these latter corks are pinned little cubes of camphor. Then the wheel is completed. Its success depends on having the various parts very accurately balanced.

Now for the fun. Half fill up a bath with cold water, place the contrivance carefully on the surface, and immediately it commences to rotate. It will continue to spin round unceasingly for a day or two, without getting giddy. When it stops, the camphor should be renewed, and then it will go on again for another day or so!

COMICAL SHADOW THEATRE

The diagram will give a good idea of how this comical shadow theatre is constructed. The frame is made of the sides of a shallow wooden box with the bottom removed. Across the back and front faces a piece of tracing linen is stretched. The figures are shaped out of thin card, and their arms are planned to move in the way that a railway signal arm moves up and down. This system may be seen in the second diagram. A thin upright of wood is fixed to the bottom edge of the theatre, and the body of the actor is glued behind it. Then a horizontal cross-piece is nailed to it at A. The cross-piece must work freely on the pivot A, and it must be so arranged that it can be raised by pulling the wire fixed at B. On this horizontal the arm of the actor is fixed, and he holds a trumpet. It must be so planned that when the wire loop is pulled the arm lifts the trumpet up to the mouth, and when the wire loop is released the arm falls down and the trumpet moves away from the mouth. The other figure works on the same system; but in this case one wire lifts or lowers his two arms. When they are raised they come up to his ears, suggesting that the trumpet makes an unbearable noise.

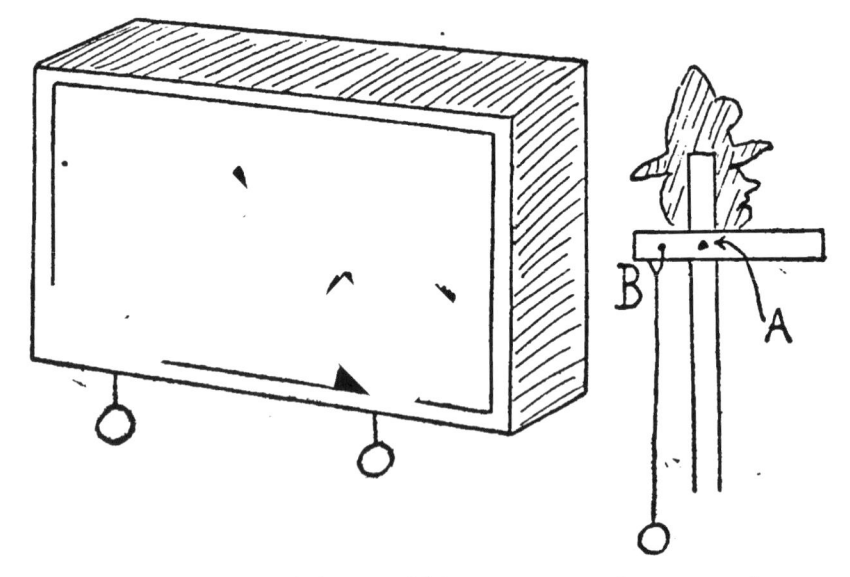

The wire loops project below the edge of the theatre. They pass through two small holes bored in the wood by means of a gimlet.

Hundreds of Things a Boy Can Make

Here only the bare outline of the shadow theatre is given. Other details will suggest themselves.

To see the figures to their best advantage place a lighted candle behind the theatre and have the room otherwise darkened.

JOLLY RAILWAY TRAINS EASILY MADE

You know how satisfactory it is to make useful playthings out of waste materials. Well, here is a capital idea which will amuse you for hours.

Railway rolling stock is rather expensive to buy in any quantity; moreover, no self-respecting person would take the trouble to play with fewer than three or four trains at a time, which means an expenditure of at least ten shillings. Now the idea is this. Spend an hour making the models described below, and spend, also, sixpence on buying a pot of paste and you will save nearly all the ten shillings just mentioned.

First, you must collect a number of empty cigarette packets of the kind that hold ten cigarettes. If your father or big brother smokes, this will be an easy matter. Get all the packets the same size and select only uncrushed ones.

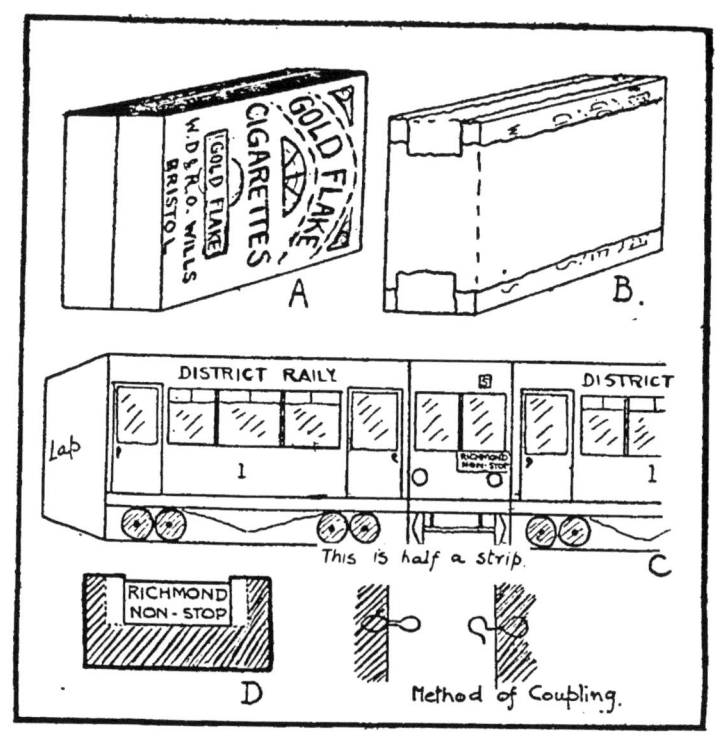

Now for business. Place the cartons in twos, side by side, standing on the long edges, as shown by Fig. A. Then, fix straps of pasted paper around them, as shown in B. This will securely hold each pair of cartons together and the pair will then serve for one coach. You will want as many pairs, so joined, as you decide to make coaches.

The next thing is to make up your mind what railway company you are going to imitate. We suggest that your trains should be electric, for then you will not require any locomotives, which are a little difficult to construct. If you go in for Southerns, your rolling stock must be coloured green, if it is " Undergrounds " you decide on, then they must be red.

We are going to suppose that your choice lies with the Underground. Get strips of white paper just the width of the two cartons and a little longer than their length. Paste them on to serve as the white roofs, and be careful to press down the extra bits on the sides. Now cut lengths of white paper long enough to wind round the sides and ends of the cartons, with a little piece to spare. On these you will draw in Indian ink and paint in red, the pattern of an Underground coach. See Fig. C. When they are quite dry, a length is pasted round each twin-carton and a fine coach it will look. Note, as we cannot trouble about actual wheels, we draw them instead. They will glide along the table quite nicely as they are.

We must not forget that the Underground people are very careful to tell passengers the destination of their trains, so we must do the same. It will be quite easy. Under the right-hand window of the front end of each train must be fixed an extra piece of red coloured paper, as shown at D. Only the shaded part must be pasted; then the " Richmond " board can be slipped in and held there. Of course, you will make a number of boards bearing different destinations, such as Ealing, Wimbledon, Barking, Mansion House, etc. With them, you will be able to have great fun in changing the route from time to time

There is just one thing more to do, and that is to provide the couplings for the coaches. If you are going to have " set " trains, stick a little bridge of paper between each two coaches, allowing four coaches to a train. But when we ourselves made some of these trains, we fixed a wire loop at one end and a wire hook at the other end of each coach. This enabled us to couple up the trains as we liked.

If you prefer to run your trains about on lines, spread some white paper on the table—we have used the reverse side of a roll of wall paper—and draw the lines on it. Think what a splendid lot of junctions and sidings you can make on it.

SIX MODEL RAILWAY ACCESSORIES

Most boys, and very often their fathers as well, are keenly interested in model railways. There is something fascinating in setting up a well-planned track with a station or two, if all the little odds and ends of equipment are available. Although we do not suggest that an average boy should make his own engines and rolling stock, we do advise him to construct many of the other things which go to make his system look realistic. Here are a few models well worth attempting.

A LOADING GAUGE

This is an arm-shaped accessory with a curved upper bar. It is placed by the side of the track and loaded trucks are passed under it. If the goods trucks can pass without touching the top bar, they will not come to grief in tunnels. Make the vertical and horizontal bars of $\frac{3}{8}$ in. quartering. Fix the angle with a screw, but after making the screw hole, and before fixing the screw, glue the join, then tighten up the screw. Support the upright on a block of wood, heavy enough to steady the arm. Cut the curved gauge out of thin sheet iron, and suspend it by looped wire.

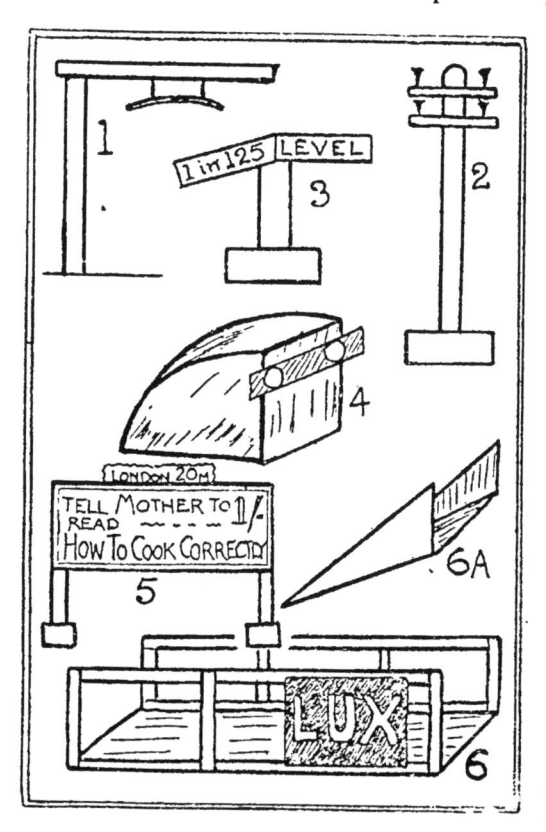

Paint the whole of the accessory white, with the exception of the bottom part, which should be black. Use oil paints, well thinned with turpentine. The height of the vertical post should be a trifle more than the height of your highest piece of rolling stock. (See Fig. 1.)

TELEGRAPH POSTS

Half a dozen of these posts will form a pleasing addition to the stock of accessories. They are easily made out of cheap wooden penholders. Fix the foot into squares of wood—we have used some derelict draughtsmen for the purpose. With a pocket-knife cut recesses for the upper cross-bar, and glue them into position. Before fixing them, however, drive in slight nails, as shown in Fig. 2, to look like insulators. Give the whole a coat of indian ink, and use black thread for the wires.

GRADIENT POSTS

These are the little posts we see at intervals along railway lines which tell the engine-driver what inclines he has to deal with. With a pocket-knife cut two pieces of wood, ⅜ inch by ⅛ inch by 1 inch. Fix them to a slightly stouter post, 1½ inches high, and pin it to a foot. Place the arms at different angles, as shown in Fig. 3. Paint the whole object white, and when perfectly dry print the levels, as shown in the figure. Make three or four of these at the same time.

BUFFER STOPS

These are absolutely necessary to any well-equipped track. Take a solid piece of wood and shape it, as shown in Fig. 4. Its width should be slightly wider than that of the track—i.e., when No. 0 gauge is used it should be a trifle more than 1¼ inches in width. Pin a horizontal lath across the face of the buffer. Colour the block black with indian ink, the lath red with red ink, and paste on two round spots of white paper to serve as the eyes.

FIELD HOARDINGS

We all know how field hoardings, seen from the train window, spoil the scenery. Nevertheless, they add a pleasing touch of realism when forming part of our miniature railroad. Two or three such hoardings can be made in less than half an hour; they look well, and there is a certain amount of pleasure in posting fresh advertisements from time to time.

Figure 5 gives a good pattern for copying. Use a sheet of cardboard, about 5 inches by 2 inches, for the poster, and support it with trestles made of wood, ⅜ inch in section. When you go on a journey by train, look out for an advertisement which takes your fancy, and draw and colour a miniature of it, when you get home, for the hoarding.

AN EASILY MADE BRIDGE

Bridges are always handy things to have. The bridge proper may be made as follows:—For the road use three-ply wood or millboard. Cut it wide enough to take a single track, and about 10 inches long. Make two skeleton parapets, and then nail them to the roadway. Fix a card here and there on the parapet and print on each the lettering of some well-known advertisement. If an incline is to be fitted to either side of the bridge, shape it out of millboard, as shown in Fig. 6A. Do not make the incline too steep.

A MODEL RAILWAY BOOKSTALL

Many boys have model railways with engines, passenger carriage, goods trucks, and track complete. For them a miniature bookstall would make a really fine addition to the station platform. To construct one is the work of an afternoon, and the cost is practically nothing.

An old cardboard box may be used for the purpose, but, as a rule, it will be better to model the bookstall out of a flat sheet of card. The shape and size can then be made according to one's wishes, and they will not have to conform to those of whatever box is available.

The size of the model depends on the uses to which it will be put.

If required to go with a No. 0 gauge miniature railway the scale will be about a ¼ inch to the foot. As a real bookstall is often 30 feet long,

Hundreds of Things a Boy Can Make

this means that the model is to be from 7 to 8 inches long. The height is about a third of the length—perhaps a trifle more will be advisable—and the depth should be from 1 to 2 inches, according to the space available where it is to stand.

First make a paper pattern of the model, to be quite certain, before cutting the card, that the fitting is correct. There will be wanted a front and a back, both of similar dimensions, two sides alike in shape and size, and a roof, but no floor. They should be cut, preferably, in one piece and folded. If all the faces are separate the making-up is far more difficult. The edges are joined together by lengths of gummed paper, such as is sold commercially for doing up packages.

Before the model is erected an opening should be cut for the counter. The counter itself is made by bending inwards a part of the card which originally filled the space of the opening.

When white card is selected for the model, it is a straightforward piece of work to paint it suitably and add whatever drawing is necessary. But if the card has done duty in some other capacity and is soiled, lettered, etc., it must be faced with white paper. This should be done before it is made up.

The stall is to be a miniature replica of a real one; accordingly it had better be coloured yellow-brown to look like grained wood and lettered along the cornice with the name of W. H. Smith & Son, or Wyman. Below the counter should be drawn a number of placards, advertising various periodicals. Fresh ones can be pasted over them whenever desired. A better plan is to bore a number of fine holes in the cardboard below the counter and to thread two parallel rows of loops, made of flower wire, through them. In this manner the placards can be held in place and renewed in much the same way as they are on a real stall.

The counter must be arrayed with miniature magazines and newspapers. Sheets of paper, cut to size and piled one above the other, will make a very good representation of actual periodicals. They should be stuck together and the top one lettered. Others may be displayed about the stall, either hanging from the inside of the cornice edge or fixed to the upright sides.

A RAILWAY TUNNEL

A tunnel makes a splendid addition to the equipment of your toy railway lines. You can make a fine specimen with very little trouble.

120   *Hundreds of Things a Boy Can Make*

First procure a thin sheet of iron and hammer over the edges so that they will not cut or scratch your fingers. Then determine the size the actual tunnel is to be. The height should be about 7 inches, whilst the width depends on whether you want it to take one or two sets of metals. Having decided these points, bend the iron as shown in diagram A, making the rises and the cross-run according to the lengths you have determined.

Next cut out of fretwood two pieces to serve as entrances to the tunnel, as shown in Diagram B. Follow this by getting some odd pieces of cloth and dip them in a very wet mixture of plaster of Paris. Take them out of the solution and arrange them irregularly over the tunnel. Keep on adding pieces of cloth until the whole of the metal is covered, and then make a thicker solution of plaster of Paris. Paint this over the cloth with a stiff brush and work it about so that the surfaces resemble little hillocks, paths, and other geographical features.

When the shaping is finished coat the surfaces with various coloured oil-paints to represent green grass, sandy paths, etc. Then colour the tunnel entrances with grey and line out the brickwork in a darker grey.

RAILROAD TRACK

If you have a set of miniature trains you could probably do with more track than you possess. Why no make some lengths on the plan described below? It has the merit of being easily constructed, of being cheap, and it resembles real railway lines—which most bought ones do not.

Get a plank of wood 2 feet long and an inch thick. For a single track, which is described here, it should be 4 inches wide. Next obtain some lengths of wood $\frac{1}{2}$ inch wide and a $\frac{1}{4}$ inch thick and cut them into pieces 3 inches long. Such wood is regularly stocked by shops that deal in strip-wood materials. Then nail the 3 inch pieces across the plank so that they play the part of sleepers. Place them all exactly parallel to one another, marking their positions on the board with a carpenter's square. Put them 1 inch apart and leave ½ inch space at both ends of the base-board. Thus sixteen sleepers will be wanted for a 2 foot length of track.

The next step is to obtain some moulding of the pattern shown in the diagram. It can be bought for three halfpence per foot. Cut it into ¼ inch lengths and use each little piece as a chair for the rails. Glue two to every sleeper, one at each end.

Follow this by getting lengths of strip-wood, two for each piece of

track. They should be 2 feet long, a ¼ inch wide and ⅛ inch thick. Run these between the chairs so that they serve as the rails. For No. 0 gauge see that they are exactly 1¼ inches apart, and wedge them tightly by knocking little blocks of wood between them and the chairs.

Now paint all the surfaces, with the exception of the rails with creosote and coat the rails with aluminium. Lastly, paint hot glue over the visible parts of the base-board and sprinkle with silver sand. You now have a most realistic piece of track.

Although we have described a one-way length, many boys will prefer to make an up and down road on the same board. In such cases the board should be 9 inches wide and all other requirements will be merely doubled.

A SPRING BUFFER STOP

This is a very useful possession for those interested in model railways. It consists of a buffer stop which arrests the motion of an oncoming engine by means of a spring coil. As it will be required to take considerable shocks, it had better be made of substantial materials. Therefore let the base be constructed of sheet iron or lead, whichever is easier to obtain. The length should be about twice the width and the width is determined by the gauge of the track in use. The track of No. 0 gauge is 1¼ inches wide and No. 1 gauge is 1¾ inches. Add an inch to each side of the track and you will have a very convenient width for the base of the buffer stop.

To support the spring coil apparatus, two trestles and a pair of lean-to pillars are needed. The pieces required for these are lengths cut from a square rod ½ inch in width. The cutting is easily done with a hack-saw; the joins are made by boring holes with a brace and bit, and nuts and bolts are used for gripping the pieces together. The diagram shows how the arrangement is to be made.

The spring coil is fitted inside a length of tubing marked A in the diagram, and a short piece of rod bearing a buffer-plate is placed partly within the tube. The lengths of tube are held firmly by running a collar of brass around them, as shown at B.

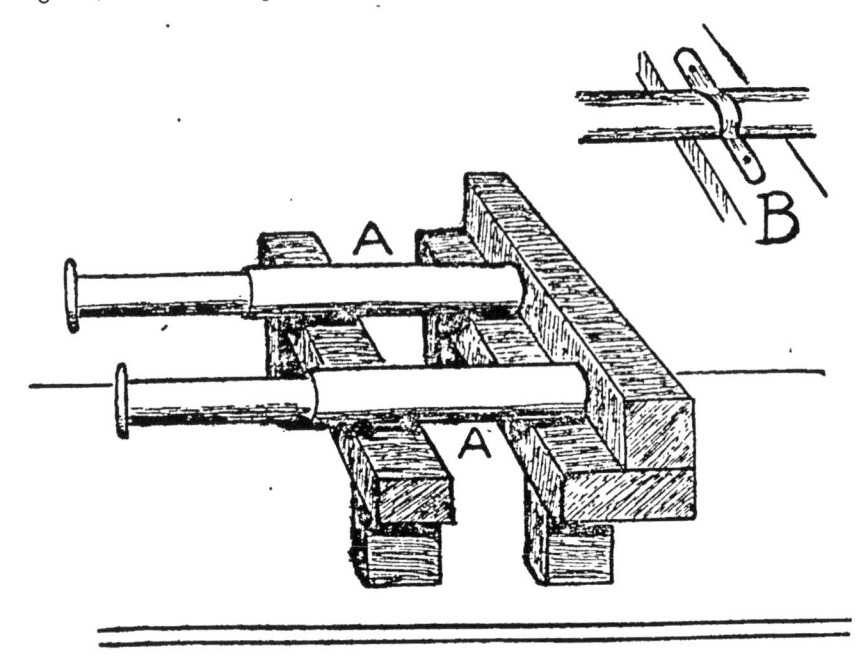

Note that only a very short piece of spring coil is required within the tube to arrest the motion of an oncoming engine. Probably, most of us will be inclined to fit far too large a piece at the outset and the effect of this will be to shoot the buffer-plate and its arm out of the tube whenever considerable compression is applied.

If the buffer-plates overhang the baseboard slightly, there will be no need to fix railway lines to the flooring; but the plates should be correctly spaced so that they are the same distance apart as those on the engines used.

SHUNTING THE TRUCKS

Here is a very jolly toy that will provide a good deal of fun and brain-racking. As you will see from the diagram, it consists of a straight piece of railway track with a curved loop line which joins the straight track at two points. In the middle of the loop there is a low bridge.

We do not suggest that you set out the track with actual miniature railway lines, although you may do so if you wish; but that you draw the track, as we show it, on a piece of cardboard and nicely colour the permanent way and the embankments.

When this is done, construct an engine and two goods trucks. Empty match-boxes will do for the bodies and paper pasted round them, suitably lined and coloured, will make them realistic enough for the purpose. Colour one of the trucks red and the other blue. In the match-box that is to be the engine wedge a piece of pencil to imitate the funnel.

There is one thing more to do, and that is to erect a bridge at the mid-point of the loop. A bent piece of cardboard will answer the purpose, if it is ornamented to look like what it is intended to be.

In constructing the bridge you must be very careful to make it so that the trucks can pass under it but that the engine cannot.

Now the game is this: Put the two trucks and the engine in the

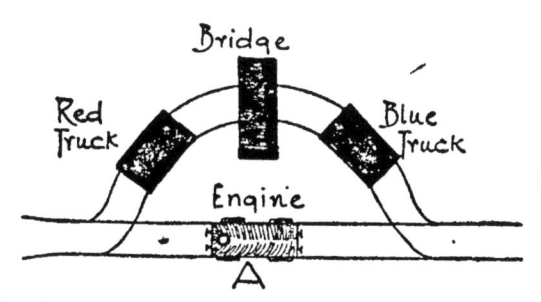

positions marked on the diagram, and then try to shunt the red truck to the position of the blue, the blue to the position of the red, finally bringing the engine back to its original station. Do not forget that the trucks can pass under the bridge but that the engine cannot.

This is the way it is done: The engine goes behind the red truck and pushes it under the bridge. It is then unhoked and comes away by itself to the blue truck, which it pushes up to the red one and brings the two down to the position marked A in the diagram. The red truck is then unhooked and the blue truck and the engine are made to travel up to the bridge, and the blue truck is pushed under it, so that it glides along to the place taken up by the red truck at the outset. The engine now comes back, takes the red truck to the original position of the blue truck, leaves it and goes to the spot marked A on the diagram.

THINGS YOU CAN EASILY MAKE FOR CHRISTMAS AND BIRTHDAY PRESENTS; ALSO TO SELL AT BAZAARS

1.—*A Smart Blotter.* Fold eight sheets of blotting paper, so that each is double the size of a piece of typewriting paper. Procure a piece of thin cardboard the same size. Cover this with pretty wallpaper, and stick down on the inside. Bind the blotting paper into the cover by threading silk ribbon through the fold.

2.—*A Slipper Box for the Fireside.* Get a box with a hinged lid from the grocer, and scrape off any paper advertisements there may be. Give a coat of spirit stain, either dark oak or mahogany, and cover the lid with a piece of sheet copper or brass, and turn over the edges. When nicely polished, this will look very attractive.

3.—*A Paper Knife.* Buy an ordinary boxwood ruler, carve it to the shape of a knife and sharpen the cutting edges. Remove all traces of the ruler with glass-paper, then ornament the handle with a poker-work design, or with bright coloured enamels.

4.—*A Sealing Wax Set.* Get an empty " fifty " cigarette box, and cover it with a smart piece of wallpaper, taking care to turn in the edges. Then buy half a dozen small Christmas candles of various colours, and trim the ends down if they will not fit long-ways into the box. Put in a partition of thin card, and in one compartment arrange the candles. In the other, place sticks of sealing wax, similarly cut down. Or you can break up the wax into short lengths, slightly warm them, and roll them into balls. If this is done, you will want a crucible. This is easily made by soldering a twist of silvered wire on to a thimble.

5.—*A Nail or Screw Box.* Get a shallow, wooden sweet box from your confectioner, but see that the bottom and sides are strong. Clean off the paper advertisements, and cover the outside with spirit varnish. Divide the inside into small compartments by means of thin wooden strips. One kind of nail or screw should be kept in each compartment.

6.—*Table Mats for Hot Plates.* Buy some thin sheet cork. Cut out some ovals or circles of thin wood with your fret-saw; face the pieces with the cork, sticking it on with thin glue. Then paint a $\frac{1}{2}$ inch border all round the edge, with one of the dyes sold for colouring straw hats.

7.—*A Window Sill Flower Box.* Measure one of your window sills—they are all made to standard sizes—and make a lidless box to fit it. Have it 8 inches high. Cover the front face of the box with virgin cork, or better still, obtain a number of square ornamental tiles, and fit them in by running a grooved moulding all round the edges. Only ornament the one side that shows.

8.—*A Wire Toasting Fork.* Buy about three-pennyworth of medium gauge wire—it will be enough for two forks—plait three strands to form a handle, and finish each strand off to serve as a prong. File the prongs to provide spiked tips. If something out of the ordinary is desired, buy from the ironmonger a wooden handle, such as is used for a screw-driver, and insert the wire into the opening provided. Smooth the handle nicely with glass-paper, give a coat or two of fixed indian ink, and rub with a piece of velvet to provide a shine.

9.—*A Box for Spare Cutlery.* Most people possess spare supplies of knives, forks and spoons which are not in daily use. A convenient box for storing these can be made out of a confectionery box, as mentioned under paragraph 5, if the inside is covered with wash leather. To stick the latter, spread tube glue thinly on the inner faces of the box, and when tacky, press the wash leather firmly on to the surfaces. Coat the outside of the box with leatherette paper, and fix on a brass catch.

10.—*A Boot Cleaning Outfit.* Take an empty biscuit tin, clean out the inside, and fit a wooden compartment large enough to take two ordinary boot brushes standing on end. These may be bought at Woolworth's for sixpence each. Coat the back of one brush with fixed indian ink, and then, in white paint, print the word " BLACK." The other brush is coloured with red ink and inscribed " BROWN." In the larger compartment, place a tin of both brown and black polish, and two pads, one for each colour. Now coat the outside of the tin with

Japan black, and when it has dried hard, which will not take long, fix a large circle of smart wallpaper on the four sides and the lid, using

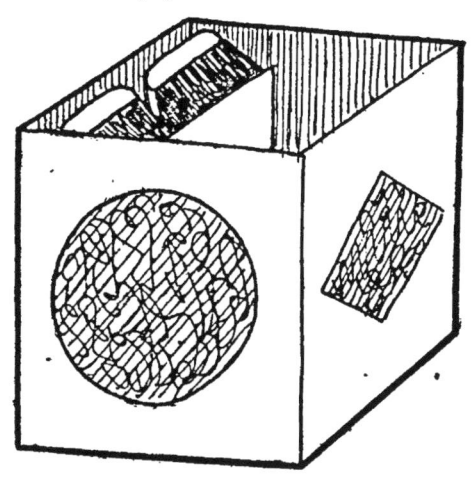

paste for the purpose. You now have an attractive and useful boot cleaning outfit.

11.—*A Newspaper Rack.* This is just the thing for those who do not like to see newspapers lying about on chairs in the sitting-room. Take two strips of wood, ¾ inch thick, and cut them as long as the *Daily Mail* is wide, and let them be about 6 inches in width. On one of the boards, fit two hooks along the top edge, to allow the rack to be hung on the wall. Fix the other board to the first along the bottom edge, so as to make an angle of about thirty degrees. The two pieces, if looked at end-on, will now appear to form an imperfect V. Cover the boards with leatherette, leather, cretonne, or anything of an artistic nature, and the contrivance will now serve to hold newspapers in a tidy fashion. If preferred, French polish the back board, and cover the front with a sheet of burnished brass.

12.—*A Novel Pin Tray.* Purchase two or three cheap pin or ash trays, wooden ones if possible. Then obtain a handful of obliterated postage stamps, take the paper off the backs, and stick them completely over the upper surface of the trays. Let them overlap in an irregular manner, and try to get different colours together. Have an attractive stamp in the centre. When they have dried thoroughly, say in two or three days, give a coat of fine size, followed by a coat of hard drying white varnish. Paste will stick the stamps on to wood, but fish glue will be needed for a celluloid surface. Score the celluloid first.

13.—*A " Hot-Cold " Container.* Your mother will find a hundred uses for this little contrivance. Get a fair sized wooden box, with a lid, and then buy a quantity of wadding and flock. Pack the flock 2 inches deep all over the bottom of the box, and on this lay a sheet of the wadding. Next, arrange a smaller box inside the larger one, so that about 2 inches are left free between them. Wrap wadding round the inner box, and wedge the sides with some more of the flock.

When you have reached to the top level of the inner box, cut a piece of millboard into a frame which will effectively hide all the flock but leave the centre box exposed. There should be at least 2 inches now between the top level of the inner box and the top of the outside box, but more will not matter.

Take two pieces of millboard, not quite the size of the big box, pack some flock tighly between them, and make them up into a sort of pillow, covered with flannel. This article should be so contrived that it will rest on the frame of millboard and fill the big box exactly. Now put a catch on the lid, to enable it to shut down tightly. This container will keep hot things hot in winter, and cold things cold in summer. Of course, you may introduce many refinements in the construction if you wish, such as fitting asbestos sheeting to the sides of the inner box.

14.—*An Unusual Money-Box.* The worst of a money-box is that you naturally want to open it to see how much there is in it, and you ought not to open it because such an act is fatal to thrift. Here is a smart little idea which gets over the difficulty.

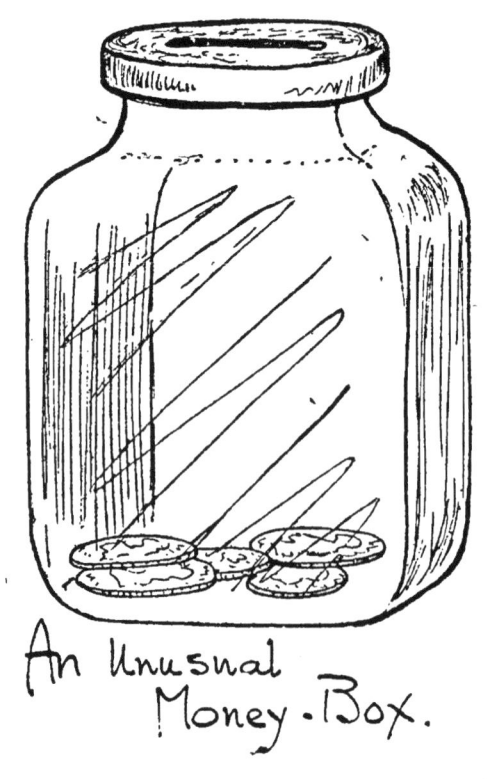

An Unusual Money-Box.

You know those glass jars with metal screw-on tops in which barley-sugar and boiled sweets are sold. Well, get one of them—empty, of course—wash the inside, and allow it to dry. In the meantime cut a straight slot in the metal lid, and, with a small file, smooth the edges and make the opening look neat. Screw on the top, coat the whole of the lid and a strip round the glass with red sealing-wax. Now it will not open without breaking the wax, and this being red it stands for " danger." Your curiosity can always be satisfied because you are able to see through the glass, and, by a little ingenuity, reckon up the extent of your wealth.

15 —*A String Cutter.* In every shop, most offices, and a good many kitchens, a string cutter is a useful tool. Make one as follows: Take a piece of wood, ½ inch thick and 6 inches square. Smooth off all the edges, and cut a V-shaped piece out of one side. Let the point of the V come a little lower than the centre of the piece of wood, and make the opening long for its width across the top. Near the botton point of the V, fix a discarded safety razor blade, by putting screws through the two holes. You now have an admirable string cutter.

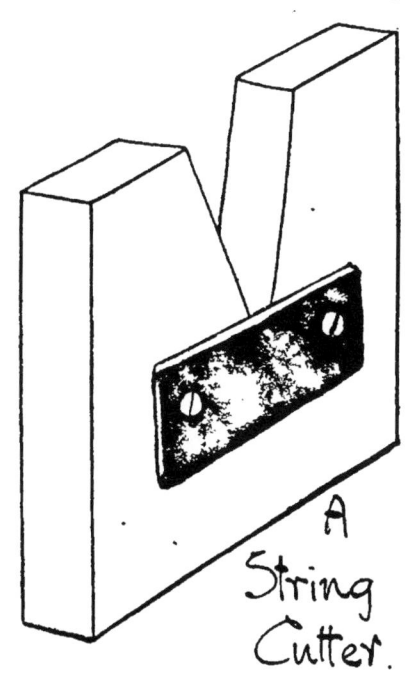

As the V is narrow, your fingers cannot be drawn on to the sharp blade, but the string easily gets there. Bore a couple of holes through the square of wood, near the two lower corners. Screws can then be slipped through them and the contrivance fixed in some handy place.

16 —*A Clip Rack.* Here is an ingenious little article with a hundred uses. Take a piece of board, say 1 foot by 4 inches, and ½ inch thick. Plane up the edges nicely and glass-paper the faces. Put a pair of hooks on the top edge, equidistant from the ends; then bore six or eight round holes through the wood. These holes must be just big enough to allow a clothes peg to be pushed through from the back, Of course, you must use the kind of peg that has a round head and a pair of long springy legs. As the legs must fit tightly, you may have to screw them in from the back. Paint the board and the pegs in jazz colours and make the contrivance look attractive. It will be useful for many purposes—as a pipe-rack, a tool rack, a rack for kitchen utensils, etc.

17 —*A Household Sharpener.* Our experience is that the people

who work in kitchens sadly neglect the edges of their cutting implements. You will find your mother, for instance, trying to cut a piece of raw meat with a knife that is only fit to deal with the proverbial lump of butter. Why not make her a kind of strop, one that she would take a pride in using?

Obtain a strip of wood, 18 inches long, 3 inches wide, and 1 inch thick. At one end, carve a flat handle and make it nice and comfortable to grip. There is now a length of about 13 inches left. Cover this, on one side, with the finest emery cloth, and on the other, with a length of good wash leather. Pin down these two materials on the thickness of the wood, not on the face of it, or you will not be able to run a blade up and down the surface. It is advisable to round off the edges of the wood; the emery and wash leather will then enjoy a longer life of usefulness. The emery will, of course, provide a fierce edge to your knife, while the wash leather will give it a proper finish. Do not use stainless or other good knives on this sharpener. It is only intended for putting a good business-like edge on kitchen knives and carpenter's tools.

18.—*Three Shies a Penny*. It is really wonderful what a lot of fun can be got out of home-made toys and games. Here is a simple little article which will provide endless fun. The ingredients in this case are one old straw hat (man's), one bottle of ink (vivid colour, red, green, or mauve), six ping-pong balls, the use of one paint-box, a piece of string, and one nail.

First you take the hat and draw out the internal lining. Next, you give the outside a coat of ink, to make it look lively. After that, you cut out an oval from the crown. This should be about 4 by 3 inches, and the crown is now painted up to look like a face, the opening being taken for the mouth. The string and the nail are used for hanging the hat on the wall. Now then, the fun begins. Take three ping-pong balls, and if you are a big chap, stand six feet away; come closer if you are small. The game is to feed the monster. His mouth is big enough.

? ? ?

This is a very wonderful piece of apparatus, yet it costs practically nothing to make.

Next time your mother plucks a chicken, save half a dozen of the feathers. You will want nice downy specimens, with the threads undamaged. If there are any slits in the delicate parts, carefully smooth them out.

Now, obtain two cards, each about 4 inches square. Find the centre of each, then draw on them a circle with a diameter of 3 inches and cut out the central part.

So far, you are probably wondering what all this will lead to. Well wait a little longer and proceed with the construction. Take one of the cards and place the feathers neatly across the opening; then glue the second card so that it overlaps the first and grips the feathers in position.

Of course, it is not easy to arrange feathers in an orderly manner; what you should aim at is to fill the whole of the circle with smooth down, without more open spaces or overlapping than is necessary.

Now for the mystery. Hold up your hand in front of an electric light bulb. Your hand merely looks a black silhouette. Place the feather grid between your eyes and your hand, and close to the latter. For some mysterious reason, you now see your hand as though it were an X-ray picture—the bones are black outlines, the flesh is semi-transparent, and so on.

THE GAME OF CORKS

Some of the simplest games provide more fun than those which are elaborate and costly. The game of corks, described here, can be made, for instance, in a few minutes, and it will afford hours of real amusement. The cost is nothing.

Get six large corks and rub them up on glass-paper so that they look neat and clean, and, above all, so that they stand firmly on their larger circular face. Now cut a little depression in the centre of each of the faces on which they are to stand, and then run a long French nail through the cork, so that it sticks up a good way above the top edge. (See diagram). The head of the nail will lie snugly in the depression and the cork will not want to topple over. On each cork write such numbers as 0, 5, 10, 15, etc. Lastly cut a dozen or more rings from post cards. The diameter of a ring should not be less than an inch and a half.

To play the game, stand up the corks in " duck formation " on the table, 2 feet from the edge. Give each player six rings at a time and see which one can, by throwing them over the spiked corks, score fifty points first.

A TOY CHEST

The worst of toys is that, unless their owners are very tidy people, the living rooms of the house are apt to be everlastingly in a state of chaos. A toy chest, however, is a great boon, and if it is a nice one that takes the eye of its young possessor, there is a real chance that all the little odds and ends of things will be put away when they are done with for the time being.

If you would like to make your small brother or sister an attractive toy chest, go to the grocer's and buy a well-made box, not forgetting that you want the wood to fashion a lid. When you have an hour or so to spare, rub all the sides of the box, both in and out, with glass-paper, make a hinged lid, and put on four small feet. We have used four cheap round drawer handles for the purpose.

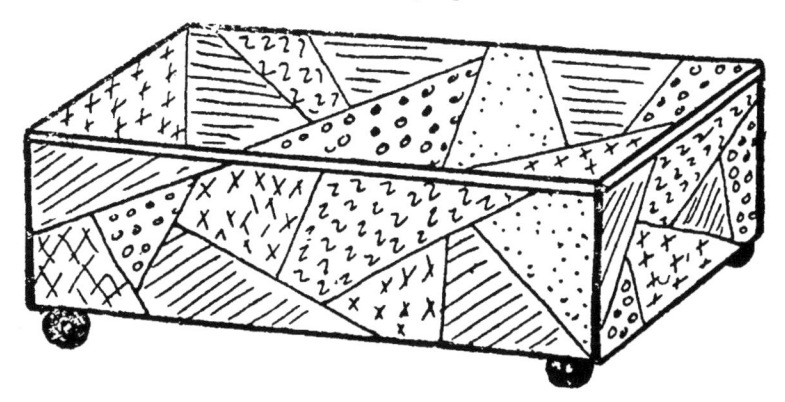

You now have to paint the chest. First give it a coat of white or cream, then when that is quite hard, with pencil and ruler divide all the outside faces into triangles and paint each a bright colour—red, blue, yellow, green, etc. See that no two adjacent triangles are of the same colour. For a few pence you have an attractive jazz toy chest.

A MUSICAL BOX

Take an empty circular blacking tin and clean out the inside; then cut three or four pieces from a length of spring ribbon, such as is used for mechanical toys. Let the pieces be about 2 inches long. Make a hole in each length, fairly close to one end. Also make three holes, equidistant, in the edge of the box part of the tin. Place the lengths of ribbon in the box and grip them to the edge by passing a tiny bolt through a hole in the tin and the hole in the ribbon, then fastening a nut on the tip. Bend the free end of each piece of ribbon in a curl towards the centre of the tin.

Now put the lid on the tin, and be sure that the spring ribbon is not too wide, to allow the lid to close properly. Follow this by boring a hole through the centre of the lid and the bottom of the box. Take a short length of rod—a long French nail with the head nipped off will do. It must be possible to slip it through the two holes just made and suitable for serving as an axle. To the centre of this axle solder another portion of a French nail, slightly less in length than the radius of the tin.

The contrivance is now assembled together. The axle end is slipped through the hole in the bottom of the box, the spoke-like part is kept within the box, the lid is replaced, and the two projecting ends of the axle are turned over to keep all the parts together. One end of the nail should project considerably more than the other, and it should be bent to form a handle.

The toy is finished—all but a coat of bright paint to make it look attractive. On turning the handle, the internal spoke comes in contact with the pieces of spring, and in passing them plucks them and makes a musical sound. If the three springs are cut to slightly different lengths the notes will be different. It is just the kind of musical box to please a small child.

THE WHIRLING TOY

Here is an easily made toy that is very amusing. First, you require a thin board, the dimensions of which matter very little; but 1 foot by 4 inches will serve quite nicely. Somewhere, not quite in the middle of the length, make a hole and glue into it a circular wooden rod, on to which you can slip an empty cotton reel. The rod must allow the reel to revolve freely on it.

Close to one end of the board, spread out a stout rubber band and tack it down, near the edge of the board by means of a U-shaped staple. The band we used served as the collar of a pot of meat paste. It can be seen in the diagram between A and B. At A a piece of string is looped; it is then wound once round the cotton spool and taken through two more U-shaped staples, seen at C and D.

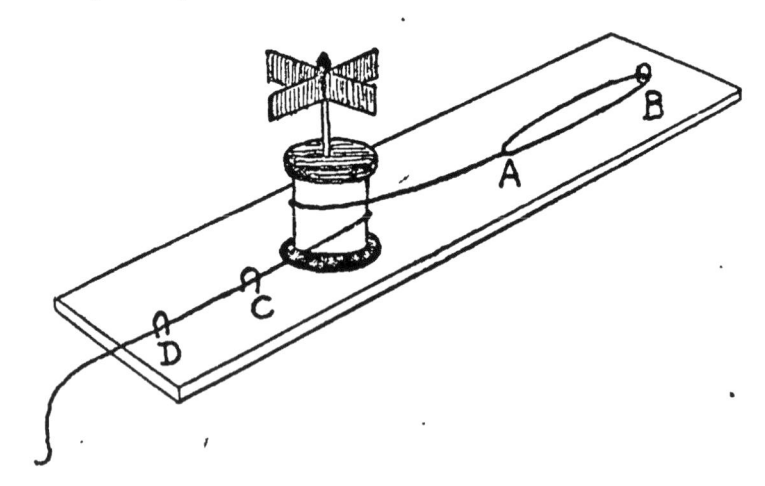

Now, this is how the toy acts. If you pull on the string, the reel revolves, owing to the elasticity of the band, A B. Of course, you must only pull a little and, then, if you release the pressure, the elastic band contracts and pulls the reel in the opposite direction. Thus, by alternately pulling and releasing the string, the reel revolves first one way and then the other.

In the top of the reel, we have erected an imitation weather vane, painted various colours; you can imitate this or put a cut-out gymnast, or anything you like, in its place.

LIGHTING UP A MOTOR BUS

Nearly every toy shop sells tin motor buses nowadays, and some of them are exceedingly faithful likeness of the real things. You can buy, for instance, a miniature " General " which is an exact replica of the leviathans running in the London streets. A small boy of our acquaintance possesses a whole fleet of them, and although he is only eleven, he conceived the idea of fitting them with electric light. We found him one evening, playing with them on the dining-room table. The room light was out, but his " Generals " were giving out sufficient to enable him to see as much as he wanted. It was, without doubt, a pretty sight. Perhaps you will want to light up a bus of your own. It is not hard, and the equipment is not expensive.

The first thing to determine is the number of lights that are to be provided. Four is the proper complement, two head-lights, one red rear light, and one front route number light. If four should be decided on, a rather large dry battery will be needed ; but should you consider two head-lights sufficient, then one ordinary battery, such as is made for pocket torches and sold at fourpence or sixpence, will be ample. Of course, it is possible to use two small batteries, and work a couple of lights off each.

Having selected the number of lights, you are ready to purchase the equipment. You will want one bulb and one bulb holder for each

Position of bulbs shown by arrows.

light, one or two batteries, and about two yards of flex, carrying a light wire.

As all the fittings are placed inside the vehicle, it will be convenient to remove the top deck by lifting up the little metal projections. They will have to be replaced when the installation is complete, so be careful not to break any of them off.

The head lights are best fitted at the front window spaces, beside the driver. If there are no such openings, they may be drilled easily. These should be about ⅜ inch in diameter. Take the two bulb-holders and fix them in the windows by means of sealing-wax. Solder would be better, but it will scorch the paint-work. Then screw in the bulbs. Now take two pieces of flex, each 3 inches long, and unwind a little of the plaited strands, also bare the wire tips by scraping away the silk and rubber covering. Fix one of the tips to the nut on the bulb holder, and the other tip to the hole in the collar. Then take the far end of the same piece of flex, and fit the two tips, one on each prong of the battery. The bulb will now light up.

As you are running two lights off the same battery, a little care must be exercised in joining up the second bulb, because the bus has a metal body and the collars are touching it. If it had been a wooden bus, the case would be different. You must have a similar arrangement for the second bulb as the first The same individual wires must be joined at the battery and at the bulb. If the wrong ones are connected, there will be no light. This will tell you plainly that your wiring is incorrect, and you must reverse it. Then the light will come on.

If there is to be a rear light and a route number light, these should be run off a second battery, and their wiring is similar to that already described, except that the wires will probably have to be a little longer.

The rear light must be red. Red bulbs can be bought, but they cost three times as much as plain ones. Therefore, you may decide to colour a white one with red ink, or, better still, with a red dye.

The route-number light goes on the under-flap of the roof above the driver. The collar is fixed high up with sealing wax, and a little cardboard frame fitted round it in which the numbers may be slipped. These numbers should be printed in white on a black ground; then they will look very realistic.

A tiny switch for turning the lights on or off may be thought necessary, but there is hardly room enough for it inside the bus. The easiest plan is to give each bulb a turn in its socket to make the necessary change. If a switch is used, all the wires must be cut longer, and brought to the switch, which is rigged up at the doorway.

When the installation is complete, the upper deck of the bus is returned to its place, all the little projections are slotted and bent over, and everything is ready for a trip at night.

THE SNAKE IN THE BOX

For this toy you will want a good strong box with a well-shutting lid. Let it be, for preference, a cube with sides 3 inches long. Next look through your tool cupboard and see if you can find a stout spring coil with a diameter of about an inch. If you cannot find one, the nearest ironmonger will supply you with one for about threepence. The coil must be one that compresses into a 3 inch space but will shoot out to at least 6 inches.

Fix this spring firmly to the bottom of the box, and be very careful that, when pressure is released, the jerk will not throw the spring from its moorings.

Now sew a piece of green cloth in the form of a tube and stitch up one end. Then draw a head on the end to resemble a snake and paint patches of yellow and other vivid colours along the entire length. Slip this tube over the coil when it is at full length, and then stitch it, here and there, so that it will not fly off.

Next compress the spring, shut down the lid, and keep it down with a hook. Then write clearly on the box, " Please do not open this," or " Mind you don't touch this hook." Of course it will not be long before some one will come along and open the box, simply because they are asked not to do so. Bang goes the coil as soon as the hook is undone and out springs the monster snake.

HOW TO MAKE A VIOLIN OUT OF A CIGAR BOX

When an itinerant musician plays an ordinary violin in the street, few people take much notice ; but let him play on an improvised cigar box, and everybody stops and listens. Apparently it is clever to be able to make and use a cigar-box violin. If it is, you can very easily become clever. We know of more than one boy who has constructed a musical instrument on these lines, and all agree that learning how to play it is the work of an hour or so.

The first thing is to get a good cigar-box, preferably one that is long compared with its width, and let it be fairly large. Remove the paper edges, if there are any, and should it be insecure at any point drive in a small nail or gimp pin to provide strength. Also, run a tiny flow of hot glue all round the inner joins to give extra strength, and also to prevent vibrations.

If the lid is hinged, do not disturb it. Cut two S-shaped openings in it, with a fret-saw, and thread glass-paper through these gaps and rub off any frayed edges.

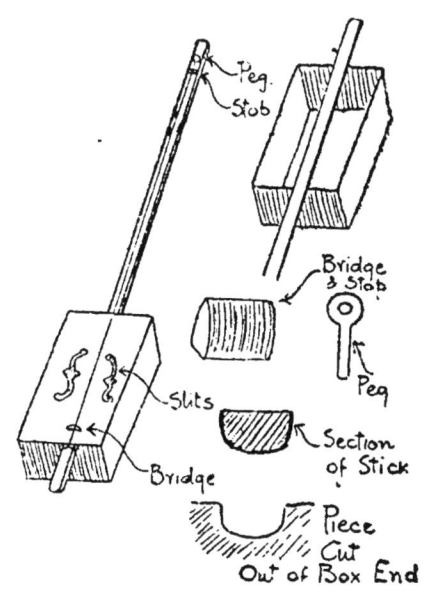

You now want a strip of wood, about 2½ to 3 feet long, and an inch square in section. Any wood will do, but it will be best to go to a shop that supplies fret-work sundries, and buy a piece of walnut. When you have it, round off two of the adjacent edges and smooth them down with glass-paper. Do this part of the job carefully, and do not be in a hurry.

The next step is to cut a little curved recess in each of the two short ends of the box, to take the rounded face of the long stick. It must lie there snugly and hold tightly of its own accord. It must also be sunk just sufficiently to fill the recess when the lid is shut down. Note carefully that the stick should project about 3 inches beyond one end of the box, and ever so many inches at the other end. When all this has been carefully thought out, the stick is glued in position, and the lid treated similarly.

At the far end of the stick, an inch from the tip, bore a hole through it, and there fix a peg with a hole in it, as shown in the diagram. Then go to a shop that sells violin strings, tell them what you are making, and ask for an A string ; but be sure to get it long enough for your violin. Ordinary violins will not need strings nearly as long. Be quite clear on that point.

When you reach home, make a loop in the string, slip it over the bottom end of the stick, run it over the cigar box and up to the peg, thread it through the hole, and twist the peg until the string makes a healthy twang. Then make two tiny V-shaped blocks out of wood, one larger than the other, and fit the larger, as shown, on the lid of the box, and the smaller up close to the peg.

Your violin is finished, and all you want is the loan of a disused bow. Sit on a stool, place the end of the stick on the floor, on your knees, or on the stool, take the bow in your right hand, grasp the upper end of the stick and manipulate the string with the left. You are now on the highroad to becoming a celebrated musician.

MUSIC HATH CHARMS

Here is a little instrument from which music, of sorts, may be evolved. Take a wooden box which is, preferably, about twice as long as wide. The depth does not matter. Along each major side nail a thin strip of wood, so that the two pieces together fill in the whole of the top opening of the box, except for a 2 inch space along the centre.

Next drive nine nails in one of the pieces of wood, spacing them in a straight line. Then drive a similar number of nails in the other piece of wood. The two rows of nails must be so arranged that they gradually grow farther and farther apart, the nearest pair of nails having a distance of $2\frac{1}{4}$ inches between them, and the farthest pair $4\frac{3}{4}$ inches. The nails, it must be added, should not be driven quite home ; they should stand up a trifle above the wood.

Now get some good flexible wire and join every pair of nails. The nine wires thus cross over the open box, and each is a trifle longer than the previous one. By giving a little care to the stringing it will be possible to make each wire emit a different musical note when it is plucked, and on this condition being produced it will not be difficult to play a tune on the wires.

A TOY WINDMILL

Never throw away the cardboard tubes in which people send things through the post, since there are dozens of models that can be made out of them. Here is one. Cut a piece from such a tube about 8 inches long, paste a covering of yellow paper around it and then draw windows here and there and add a doorway. Somewhere near the top force a knitting needle through the card and push it along until it penetrates the card on the other side of the circle. Withdraw the needle and two holes appear. Through these holes thread a piece of stout wire. At one end twist the wire to make a handle, and at the other leave just sufficient length to support a cork. The cork should have four slits made in the sides, and in these are forced the tips of four strips of thin card, previously shaped to look like the sails of a windmill. When the cork is fixed to the end of the wire and the handle is revolved, the windmill will sail gaily round and round.

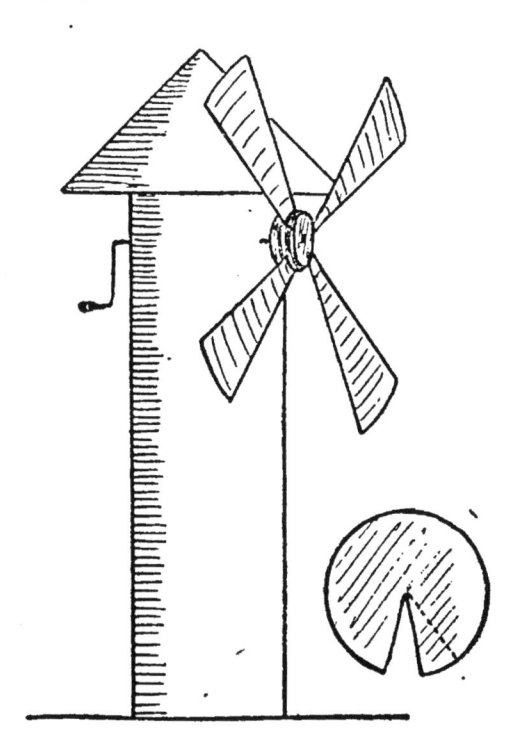

It will add to the appearance of the mill if a pointed roof be supplied. Draw a circle, paint it red, or some other attractive colour, and then cut it out; but cut, also, a piece out of the circle, as shown, then join up and the flat paper becomes tent-shaped. A touch of glue or paste will hold it in position.

THE ROCKING NIGGER

This is, really, a very silly thing: but it provides a good deal of amusement and it will, probably make you laugh.

Draw and colour a nigger boy's head, about 4 inches high, on a stout piece of cardboard and cut it out. Then trim up a piece of wood to the shape of a cube, having a side about 2 inches. Fasten the head to one of the faces of the cube and, in the opposite face, drive in two large cut nails. Snip off the heads of these nails and force in the headless ends. The cube will then stand on the points of the nails. In arranging the position of these two nails, be very careful to see that they are placed on an imaginary line, joining the middle point of two opposite edges of the face of the cube. Next, obtain a piece of stout wire, about 2 feet long and bend it, as shown in the illustration. Force one end into a side face of the cube and, at the other end, attach a small weight, such as a lead weight used by anglers.

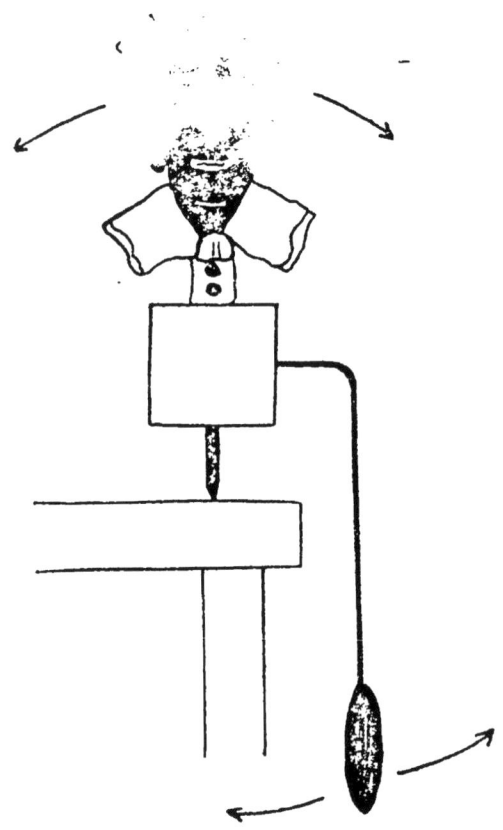

Now stand the little device close to the edge of a table, give it a push sideways and Mr. Niggerboy will sway his head from side to side, for a considerable while.

A NOISY RATTLE

You love to make a noise, of course. Here is something with which you can rouse the whole household. Get as large a cog-wheel as you can. It is not a very easy thing to make, so we commandeered one from a Meccano outfit. Perhaps you would like to do the same. Through the centre of the wheel fit a 10 inch dowel rod that wedges tightly. If necessary, fit it with a small screw or pin.

Next cut two thin pieces of wood about 5 inches long, $2\frac{1}{2}$ inches wide at one end, and $1\frac{1}{2}$ inches wide at the other end. Round off the corners. Pierce the narrow end of each piece so that it slips easily on to the dowel rod, one above and the other below the fixed cog-wheel. So that they do not slip out of position, bore through the rod above and below the flaps and put in a tight peg.

Next fix a block of wood between the two flaps, at the end away from the cog-wheel, and nail it so that the flaps are kept rigid.

Lastly, on one face of the block screw a piece of steel spring, taken from a disused mechanical toy. It should be just long enough to reach

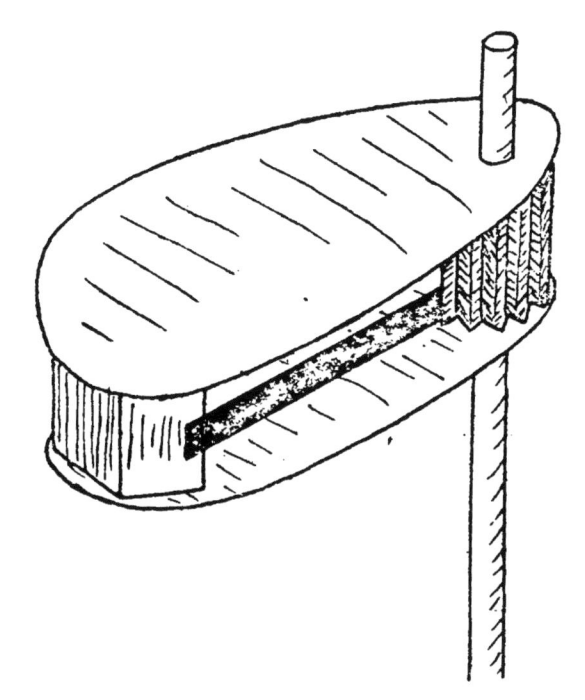

the recesses of the cog-wheel, and it must pass diagonally between the two flaps.

The contrivance is finished. Hold it firmly, give it a gentle rotatory movement, and every one within earshot will wish you were not so handy at making things.

THE GOLDFISH AND GLOBE

Here is an amusing toy which can be made in a few minutes. Procure a piece of cardboard, about 3 inches long by 2 inches wide, and white on both sides—a piece of a postcard will do. On one side of the card draw a globe such as goldfish live in, but have it quite empty of fish.

You may scribble a few lines to suggest that there is water in it if you like. Now, turn the card over so that the blank side is uppermost. In doing this be careful to see that the globe is turned upside down. On the blank side draw, neatly, a goldfish. Do it in red ink if you used black for the globe. Lastly, make two tiny holes in the sides of the card and thread them with fine string as shown in the illustration.

Hold the string taut, one end in each hand between the thumb and first finger, and rotate the card. As the card flies over, the eye obtains the impression that there is a globe with a goldfish in it.

Instead of the globe and fish, all sorts of variations can be devised, such as a canary and a cage, or your own name with alternate letters on one side of the card and the remaining letters on the other.

THE FISH GLOBE

Look at the diagram. The central line shows part of the twisted rod of a sixpenny Archimedean drill. A stout length of tubing, AB, which is an easy fit for the central rod of the drill, has a tin fish soldered to the tip of it. At B, there is a washer resting on a large band of tin, ½ inch wide. The band fits on to the central rod, two holes at B and F permitting it to do so. These holes must be exactly the same size and shape as that in the spool which is sold with the drill and which runs up and down the twisted rod. As a rule, the shape of this hole is similar to that shown at E.

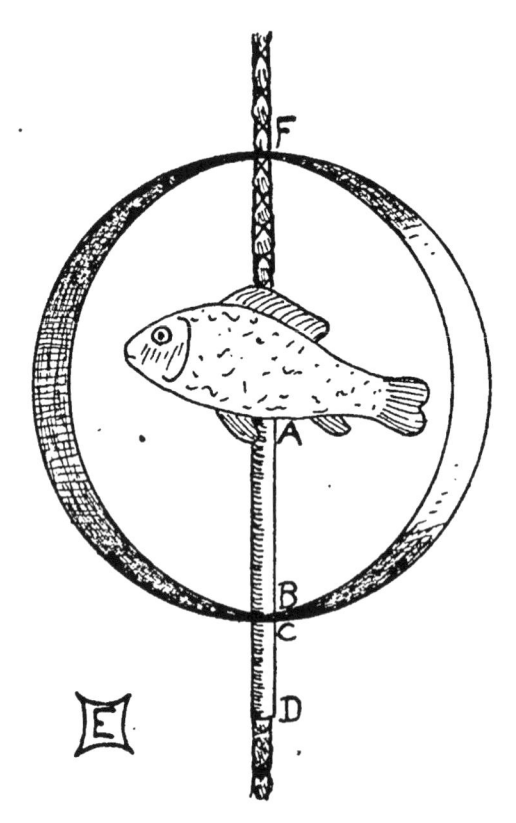

CD is a second tube, similar in gauge to AB, but it need not necessarily be the same length.

Now, this is how the contrivance works. The arrangement which you have made is dropped on to the spool, lying at the bottom of the drill. The drill is held vertically and the spool is raised and lowered a number of times in rapid succession. As it moves, it swings the band of tin round and round so speedily that your eye sees not a band but a silvery transparent ball which gives the impression that the fish is in a glass globe.

A MARBLE BOARD

Every boy likes to play marbles occasionally. Here is a splendid way to make the game even more interesting. Get a piece of wood about 15 inches long, 4 inches high, and any convenient thickness. Mark off one of the longer sides into inches and cut out seven of the alternate spaces, making them 1 inch square. Then cut two triangles

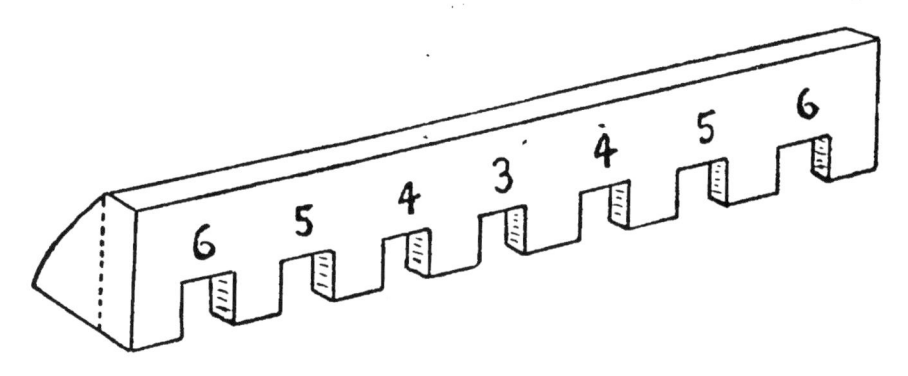

of wood and screw or nail them to the short sides of the board. The board will now stand up.

The next step is to cover the board with some bright-coloured cellulose paint and, when dry, to print a number over each opening. Put 3 over the centre opening, 4 on the openings on either side of the 3, 5 on the openings on either side of the 4, and so on.

In playing, your friends roll their marbles up to the board, and those which go through an opening have to be paid as many marbles as is indicated over the opening. Those which do not roll through an opening are claimed by you.

SIX MODEL TOWN ACCESSORIES

Your younger brothers and sisters and perhaps you as well, derive endless amusement by building model towns on the playroom table. You probably have toy houses, toy motor-cars and a host of other things, but no matter how rich you are in these possessions more miniature accessories are always welcome. There is an almost endless variety of things which you can make for the toy town. Below we describe six such articles, but each one is merely a type of many others, and the following suggestions should help you to add quite a considerable number of things to your miniature town.

PILLAR-BOXES

Every street along which your motor cars career should be furnished with a pillar box. This is how you can make four in less than one hour. Cut four pieces off an old broom handle, each 3 inches long. Then give them a domed top, by rubbing them on glass-paper. Next, cut a recessed ring all round the tops with the aid of a pocket-knife, and with the same implement cut out a space for taking the letters. Rub

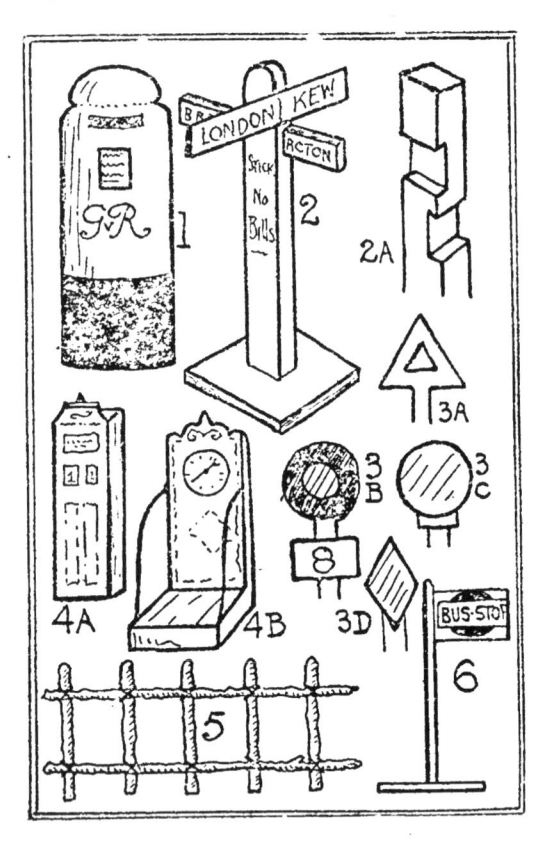

each article nicely smooth, especially the base, with fine glass-paper, and then give a coat of vermilion red. If the wood is fairly bright and clean, water colours will do, but, should it be soiled and black, oils must be used. When dry, paste on a little rectangle of white paper to serve as the time plate; then print the cypher, G.R.V., in black, and run a ring of black ink or paint round the foot of the pillar-box.

SIGN POSTS

A sign post gives a very realistic touch to the centre island at cross roads. For this little device you will want a 3 inch length of wood with ⅜ inch section. Screw it on to a flat foot of wood, but recess the screw head. Now trim up two laths, each 2½ inches long, and fit them into the centre post, as shown in Fig. 2A. Use either tiny fret pins or glue. Give the whole article a coat of white paint, and paste on to the horizontal arms pieces of paper bearing the names of places situated in your locality. Print as neatly as you can.

Make another post, with two arms only, bearing the words, "No Thoroughfare."

MOTOR SIGN POSTS

You will want some of these. Make them as directed for sign posts, but cut the indicator discs out of stout card, faced with white paper, and paint on them the necessary colours and information. Fig. 3 shows the four kinds most in use. A is a red triangle with white centre; it is placed at the approach to dangerous corners. B is a white ring; it limits the speed to ten miles or less per hour. The number of miles allowed is printed on the disc below the ring. C is a solid red disc; it prohibits the passage of cars. D is a disc which bears any notice, other than the above, to which the attention of motorists is to be called.

AUTOMATIC MACHINES

These ubiquitous machines are very interesting to make. Fig. 4A shows a kind easily constructed. It consists of a length of wood, 3 inches by 1 inch by 1 inch. Rub it smooth with fine sand-paper, and give a coat of red or green enamel, and when dry fix three small white labels to resemble enamel plates; then add suitable printing and ornamentation.

Fig. 4B shows a weighing machine. Shape the platform and upright out of wood, but use stout wire for the side arms. Pierce the wood with an awl, thread the wire through and flatten it on the back and undersurfaces so that it will not pull out. The weighing dial should be drawn on a circle of paper.

RUSTIC FENCES

These are useful for a host of different purposes. Get a number of fairly straight twigs from the garden and make them into 6 inch lengths, as shown in Fig. 5. The temptation is to use clumsy pieces of twigs, but each bar should be proportionate to the length of the fencing. As this kind of wood will not take nails, the joins must be bound tightly with flower wire.

BUS AND TRAM STOPS

These are easily made on the lines suggested for sign posts, but the inscribed part should be cut out of thick card and nailed to the upright with fine fret pins. The colour and lettering should be made to imitate the "stops" actually used in your own district.

THE DANCING DARKIE

This tireless individual is really a very funny little chap, for he cuts such curious antics. You can make him quite easily out of stiff, smooth cardboard. There is no special need to draw him exactly as we have done, and it is quite likely that you will prefer to think out a design of your own. But, generally speaking, it will be advisable to shape the head and body in one piece and each arm and leg in two pieces.

The hinges can be made of small bent pins, or perhaps you will decide to use thin flower wire. Note how the string is arranged or the little fellow may refuse to throw out his arms and legs when you pull on it. In the diagram we have shown the string on the front of the figure, in order that you may see it properly. It will do there quite well; but it makes a neater finish if put on the back, in which case the arms and legs must be on the back also.

Of course you will colour him up nicely and make him appear really attractive. What do you think of yellow legs and a blue coat or one leg and the opposite arm green, the other leg and arm red, and the body half red and half green?

MAKING OPTICAL ILLUSIONS

It is a well-known fact that the eye can be cheated, and a good deal of amusement may be derived by drawing diagrams which mislead our vision. We give here six sets of pictures which are purposely arranged so that, on looking at them, we jump to the wrong conclusion.

Take, for instance, A and B. Here we have two strips cut from a circle. Which is the longer piece? Naturally, you immediately say, "Both the same," merely because you have been asked. Your eye, however, told you it was A. In spite of what your eye told you, the truth is B is the longer. Cut out of thin card two strips like these, and get your friends to tell you what they think.

Look at C. This diagram contains a number of vertical lines. They seem to bulge outwards, yet they are quite upright. The diamond spaces placed across them give them the bent appearance.

Now take D and E. Which is the larger space? E looks much more expansive, yet they are identical in size.

Hundreds of Things a Boy Can Make

F and G are two more deceptive diagrams. F looks tall and G seems wide. Their boundaries are both squares, however.

H and I are old friends, largely because they are about as deceiving as they can be. Which has the longer vertical line? I, without a doubt seems the longer; yet it is shorter than H.

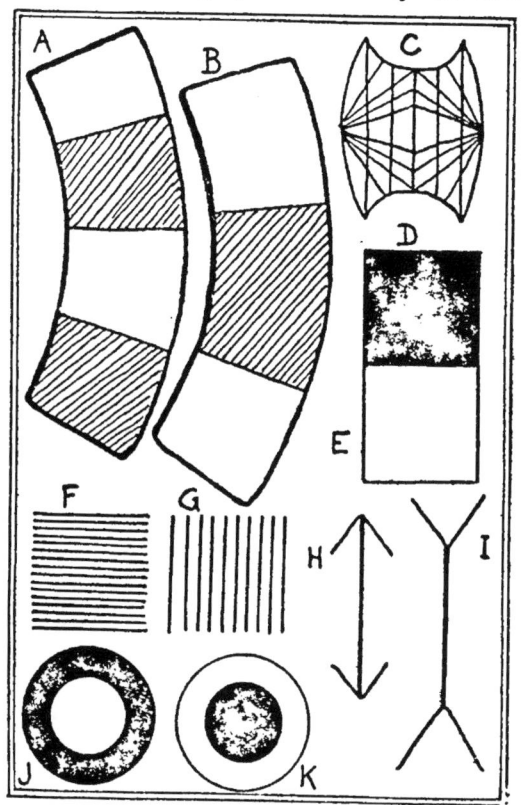

What of J and K? Would the black space of K cover the white spot in J? In spite of what your eye says, they are exactly the same size.

Draw all these diagrams on separate cards, and show them to your friends. Take F and G, for instance here they are too close, which makes them easier to judge. But on separate cards, placed a little way apart, they become far more deceptive, and this is what you want.

A DUMMY BLACK-LEAD

Take an ordinary black-lead pencil and note where the wood is joined. You can tell by looking at the untrimmed end. Then with the point of a pocket-knife carefully force the two strips apart. Another way is to soak the pencil in water, when the two pieces will become unglued. The only drawback with this method is that the water is apt to spoil the look of the pencil, and that should be avoided if possible.

When the pencil has been separated, pick the lead out of its groove, and in its place stick a length of round rubber. Select rubber of suitable diameter. Then glue the two pieces of wood together. Carefully cut the rubber flush with the untrimmed end, and at the trimmed end shape the rubber to a point.

Wait till someone asks you to lend him or her a black-lead pencil; then get out the rubber-filled pencil and watch the fun.

A REVOLVING CARDBOARD TOY

Take a rectangle of cardboard, say, 5 inches by 3½ inches, and another piece of board circular in shape, with a diameter of 3 inches. On the circumference of the round piece, draw an endless ring of people walking

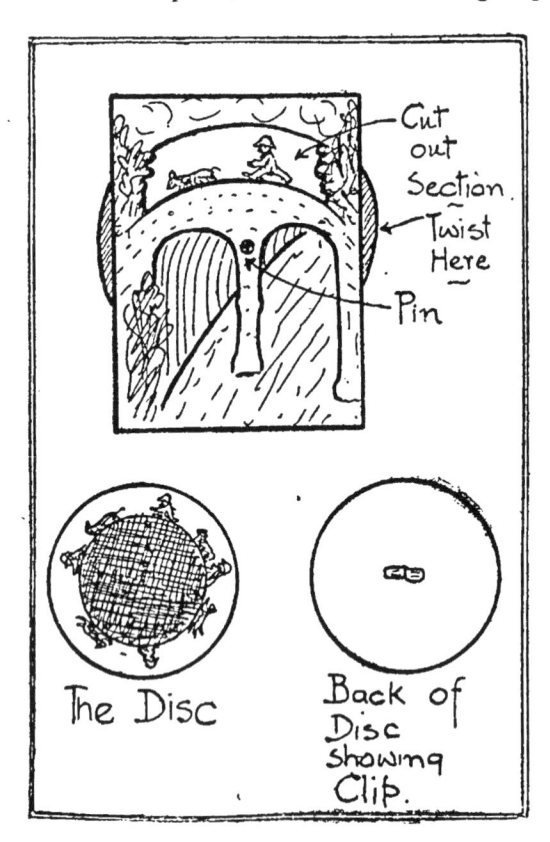

along. Cut out a small opening in the rectangular card and pin the two together with a paper fastener. By revolving the round card at the back, the people come into view and pass out of sight.

The above description tells how to make the toy, but a few additional hints may be given. First, arrange the opening with curved top and bottom so that it fits the curve of the circular card, and arrange for the opening to be at least 2 inches long. On the fixed card draw a landscape scene, and make the lower curve look like a hill or a bridge. Paint the picture if you can.

Of course there is no need to draw people walking if you prefer something else. Perhaps you would rather sketch a number of motor buses chasing each other, or a boy running after a dog. If so, do not put al

THOSE ROVING EYES

Here is one of those silly little things which cause a good deal of amusement. On a stout envelope draw a head as large as you can make it. Let it be the classic features of Charlie Chaplin, a hungry alligator, a mischievous monkey, or anything you like. Colour the features, and slit the envelope above the head and below the neck. Also cut out rather large holes for the eyes. Next take a strip of paper, just wide enough to pass through the envelope, and about 8 inches long. On the strip draw two thick, wavy, zig-zag lines, but see that the lines are always in view through the eyeholes, when the paper is drawn through the envelope. Paint the strip pink, red, yellow, blue, and green, but let one colour merge into the next. As the paper is drawn through the envelope, the lines will give the effect of moving eyes, and their movements will prove extremely funny.

MAKING A UNION JACK

Everybody should possess a Union Jack to fly on occasions of national celebrations. Those made of bunting are the most serviceable, but, being expensive, good coloured linen or casement cloth of the correct shades will do instead. A deep blue, a pure white, and a vermilion red are required.

As the setting of the flag is not too simple, we suggest that a full size plan should, first, be made on paper. Determine the length the Jack is to be, and then note the following official dimensions:

1. The red centre cross of St. George is, in width, one-fifth the long length of the flag.

2. The white edging to the above cross is one-fifteenth the long length of the flag.

3. The diagonal red cross is one-fifteenth of the long length of the flag.

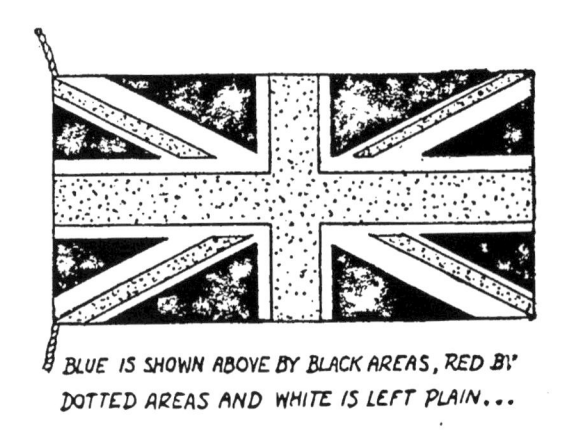

BLUE IS SHOWN ABOVE BY BLACK AREAS, RED BY DOTTED AREAS AND WHITE IS LEFT PLAIN...

4. The narrow white edging to the diagonal red cross is one-thirtieth of the long length of the flag.

5. The wide white edging to the diagonal red cross is one-tenth of the long length of the flag.

6. The deep blue material fills the remaining spaces.

Cut out the material with the aid of the paper pattern, but allow sufficient for the seams, which should be neatly ironed flat when the sewing is finished. Fix a short length of cord to the two left-hand corners to allow for hoisting.

Do not try to draw the flag from memory, unless you are perfectly certain of its peculiarities, but refer to the accompanying diagram.

GOGGLES

If at any time you want to startle your friends by appearing ugly—only temporarily, of course—put on a pair of goggles made as directed below. Your expression will be past all describing.

Get a piece of very thick card and cut it to the shape of two circular frames for the eyes, with a nose-bridge between. Let the circles be very large, but the bridge should fit the width of your own nose. Now obtain some pieces of transparent celluloid or similar transparent material. Cut four circles, each equal to the outside measurement of the cardboard circle, and glue or bind one transparent disc to each eyehole.

The next thing is to get two linen buttons much smaller than the circles of the eyeglasses. Decorate these buttons to look like a pair of glaring eyes; then put them, pattern side outwards, one on each of the fixed transparent discs, and glue on the two remaining discs. The thickness of the cardboard frame separates each pair of transparent discs by an appreciable amount, and this allows the linen button to rove about within in a most disconcerting manner.

All that remains is to fit a pair of side ear-pieces, made of cardboard, and you can proceed to startle your friends.

FUNNY FACES

Try your hand at drawing funny faces, but do it in the following way: Take a sheet of paper about the size of this page; fold the top edge over to the bottom edge and cut along the crease. Then take the two sheets and double them so that one side lies over the other. You now have a little booklet of four sheets.

With a pair of scissors cut all the pages of the booklet into four equal horizontal strips, but do not run the scissors quite up to the folded edge of the pages. Leave about an eighth of an inch uncut so that the booklet cannot fall to pieces.

Now draw a funny face on each of the four sheets, but do it in this way: arrange for a hat in every case to fill up the top space; for the face to take up the next two spaces, the eyes and nose being on the one above, and the mouth and chin on the one below; then, on the lowest space of all, have the shoulders. See that the drawings come centrally.

By turning over the flaps at random a change of face appears and the variety of expressions is endless.

It adds to the finish of the little booklet if it is pinned or sewn together along the hinged edge.

THE WOMAN WHO WALKS

Here is a toy that some young person will appreciate. Draw and then brightly colour a girl or woman on a sheet of stout cardboard, making her about 12 inches high. If you are not good at drawing people, look through some of your picture books and copy one of the people found therein. A little Dutch girl, for example, would serve admirably. When you have done this, cut out the figure. Next, take a circle of cardboard, about 5 inches in diameter, divide the circumference into six, and draw a foot in each space in such a way that the sole of each shoe is on the circumference. Cut out the shoes and a little of the stockings carefully, and pin this card with a paper fastener to the back

of the skirt, so that as the circle is revolved two little feet are always in view.

Lastly, make a handle with a thin flat stick, about 2 feet long, and glue it behind the shoulders at an angle of 45 degrees. As the stick is pushed, the figure will walk along the ground.

NOTE.—If you can do fret-work, the model will last much longer when the circle of feet is cut out of thin wood.

MUSICAL GLASSES

At some time or other you must have noticed how musical is the sound which is emitted by an ordinary glass tumbler when it is smartly tapped. And perhaps you have also noticed that two tumblers, apparently alike in all respects, will produce sounds different in tone, though both pleasant to the ear. These facts can help you to make a very charming musical instrument.

Obtain a number of tumblers; thirty-three will provide you with a full range of sounds, but you can easily do with less, say ten. Place the glasses on a flat board, preferably supported on a trestle rather than on a table. Test the sound of the glasses by striking them, and arrange them in an ascending scale of tones. Remember that a glass containing water gives a different note to that which it produced when empty. Thus, certain sounds may be obtained by partly filling a glass, and the full scale of notes is, therefore, possible by the use of empty and partially filled glasses. You will now be able to play simple tunes.

Note that the tumblers must be stood so that they do not touch, and it is well to remember that a metal tray helps to produce a far clearer tone than, say, one made of wood or covered with linoleum.

THE DOG FIGHT

As a rule we are not keen on seeing dogs fight; but in this case it is different and we shall probably enjoy it. The fight can be arranged easily. First copy the diagram of the headless dogs on a sheet of thick paper and put in any little details that may be thought attractive. Then

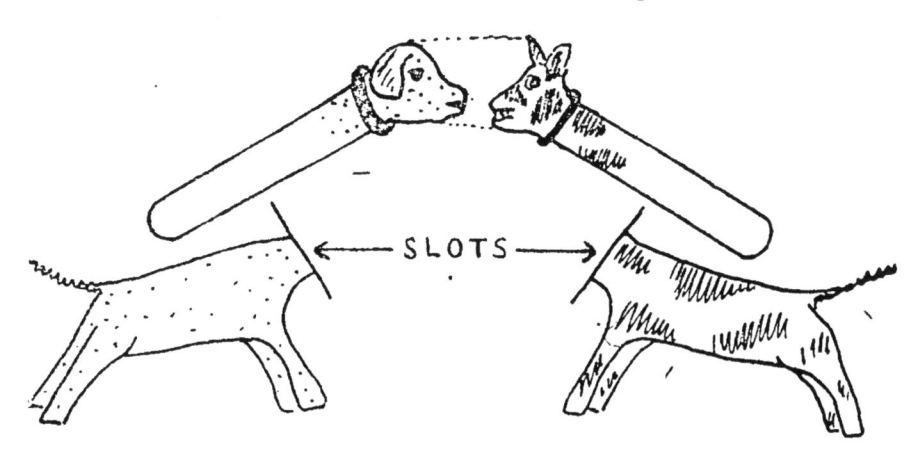

draw the two heads, and do not forget to give them long necks, as shown. By the way, the two heads must not be separated. Cut them out together and make two slots in the diagram of the bodies. Then slip in the necks and the heads will fit the bodies. By rocking the necks to and fro, when the paper is stood upright, the animals will appear very fierce. It would not be a bad idea to colour them.

A HOME-MADE PEA-SHOOTER

There are times when a pea-shooter will provide a good deal of sport All sorts of things can be used as the tube, if a real shooter is not handy but one can be made quite easily by rolling up a length of stout paper. To do the rolling neatly, wind the paper round a pencil, preferably a blue pencil, because it is usually stouter than a black-lead. Stick a piece of stamp-paper on the ends to stop them uncurling, and, if the paper has been wound diagonally, cut off the pointed tips.

Do not put the peas in your mouth, as that is very dangerous, but feed them one at a time into the tube while it is held vertically. Put your thumb at the end to prevent the charge from rolling out, and when about to blow just remove the thumb.

THE SACK MYSTERY

Are you any good at sewing? If so, you will find the *Sack Mystery* a very fine item to add to your programme of magic.

What you want is a sack large enough to envelop you comfortably, when you are crouching down. As you will most likely perform these mysterious acts when wearing your best clothes, an ordinary sack is not what is wanted. It is too fluffy, and it will make you in a mess. The best thing is to buy a piece of calico, cretonne, or similar material, and to sew up two sides to make the proper shape. Around the top edge, sew on some large brass eyelets—one every three or four inches—and then cut away the material in the centre of the eyes. After that, thread a piece of stout cord through the holes, but see that the cord will run through the holes easily.

Now, this is the trick. You collect your friends around, get into the sack and crouch down. Tell them to draw the material well over your head, then pull the cord tightly and tie it with a dozen or more knots.

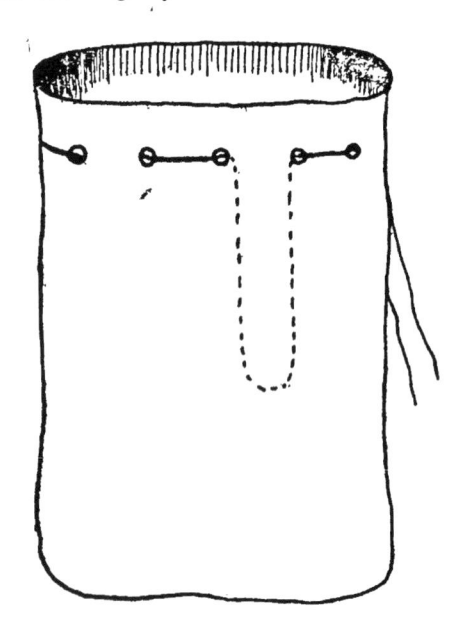

Having done this they are to leave you alone in the room for one minute, and by the end of that time, you will free yourself and emerge from your imprisonment.

It all sounds something like the wonderful tricks Houdini used to perform; but it is quite simple. The cord is much longer than it appears to be, and when you get into the sack, you pull down a long length of the slack and hold it with a finger. The diagram shows, by means of a dotted line, how the cord appears on the inside.

When your friends bunch up the opening and tighten the cord, you hold on to the slack part and this provides you with sufficient length to emerge from your prison, as soon as the room is empty.

Mind, you have only a minute, so act quickly, jump out of the sack, and with a pair of scissors which you have been careful to secrete in a pocket, cut off the knots and disarrange the cord so that the loop is obliterated. Place the short knotted length of cord in a pocket and call in your friends.

The piece of cord, which you cut off, should approximate the length of the loop. Your friends can then examine the sack and there will be no clue whatever to help them in solving the mystery.

AMUSING RINGS

Take a strip of paper about a foot long and an inch wide. *Passepartout* binding will serve admirably for the purpose. Then show it to your friends and explain to them that you are going to join up the ends and cut the paper lengthwise down the middle. Ask them what you will have as a result. The answer usually comes, without hesitation, " Why, two rings, of course."

Having been told this, you stick the two ends together ; but, while nobody is looking, you give the length one twist before bringing the two tips into communication. Then you proceed to cut the ring along the centre. It will be convenient to begin the cutting by forcing the blade of a pocket-knife through the paper and then continuing with scissors.

What have you at the finish ? Not two rings as everybody expected, but a large ring, twice the size of the one first made.

Now repeat the operation and, of course, your friends will expect to find one large ring at the finish, as before. But this time give the length of paper two twists before joining the tips ; you will finish with two rings, one linked into the other.

THE CAPACIOUS WINE BOTTLE

Here is another good trick that can be performed with a magic wine bottle. Let us suppose you are entertaining a few friends and want to mystify them. You take what looks like an ordinary dark-coloured wine bottle, and, removing the cork, pour out a glass of sparkling wine ; it is really cider, which resembles wine. If you like, you can drink it, or perhaps only take a sip. At any rate, your friends will associate the liquid, in their minds, with the contents of an untampered bottle, if you do make some show of drinking.

On putting down the glass, you pick up the bottle once more, and, while distracting the attention of your audience by saying " That was very refreshing," you snatch at an unseen thread of paper, jutting out from the neck of the bottle and withdraw yards and yards of coloured streamers, which you throw about the table and the floor.

The whole thing is so ludicrous that it cannot fail to please even the " grown-ups."

This is how the trick is done : You know that all port wine bottles possess a domed foot. Well, at the apex of the dome, drill a fairly large hole with a file, then fit a tube just wide enough to take the paper streamer. Hold it in position at the bottom by means of a thick deposit of sealing wax.

The tube must be less in diameter than the neck of the bottle, so that the liquid may be poured in and emptied out. It should reach up, through the bottle to the neck, but must not be so long that the cork cannot be inserted.

The coil of coloured paper is placed snugly in the domed compartment, at the base, and is brought up, through the tube, to the neck. The tip of it should be blackened, so that it shall not be conspicuous. It is necessary to paste a circle of black card under the dome, to keep the coil from falling out of position.

YOUR TELEPHONE

Handy boys are always making something fresh, and it is marvellous, too, what many of them can construct. The other day a boy of our acquaintance showed us a telephone that he had made with his own hands. It is such an ingenious piece of work that we will describe it for the benefit of others. First, let us say that he spent much of his time in a little workshop in the garden, and the apparatus was rigged up to enable his mother to call him indoors without having to go out into the open.

He obtained two wooden boxes—they were Tate's sugar boxes in his case—then he bought two bladders from the local butcher, and finally enough copper wire to join up the two stations. The boxes are required to be stood on end. The end that then becomes the top had a circular opening cut out of it, about six inches in diameter. This was done by marking the circle in pencil, then carefully removing the pieces of wood forming the top, cutting them along the pencil lines with a key-hole saw, and refitting the pieces to the box. This was done to both the boxes.

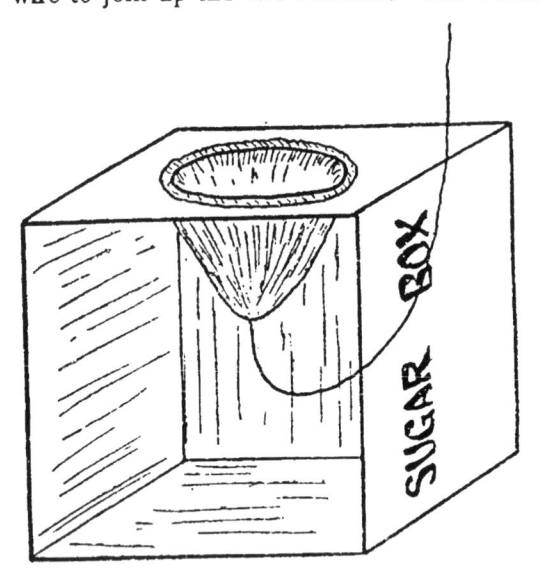

Next, he took the bladders, washed them inside and out in warm water to which was added a little lysol. Almost any disinfectant will do, if used weak. Following this, he cut off a little of the necks, where they were tied up, and then took each and spread it over the opening in the wood of one of the boxes. The diagram will show just how they looked. To keep the bladders in position, it was necessary to tack them to the wood, but there was a fear that the parchment-like substance would split ; so, to prevent this he cut strips out of an old felt hat and put them on the bladder edging, and drove the tacks through the felt, then through the skin, and lastly into the wood. This overcame all the obstacles.

The bladders being wet, there was a fear that they would shrink as they dried. To prevent this, he took a round disc of lead, about the size and thickness of a penny, punched two holes in it, threaded wire through them, passed the wire through the lowest part of the bladder, and, underneath, fixed a weight on to the wire. He did this to both the contrivances, and then left them to dry for a few days. When the bladders had dried without any cockles or creases, the weights were removed.

One of the boxes was taken to the shed in the garden and the other placed in position in the house. Then the long length of copper wire was made to connect the two ends of wire perforating the bladders. It would have been sufficient to have twisted the wire-ends together, but the boy found that, by soldering the joins, the signals were far louder.

When using the telephone, it is only necessary to bend the head over the box and speak into the bladder.

AN EASILY-MADE ESCALATOR

An escalator is something of a novelty which will add a touch of reality to many of your games with miniature models. The requirements are a cardboard box, some corrugated paper, two empty cotton reels, two blacklead pencils, and some pieces of rubber.

The diagram will show you how to plan the model. The shape of the cardboard box which you select will determine the various measurements; but it is advisable to choose one that is about twice as long as

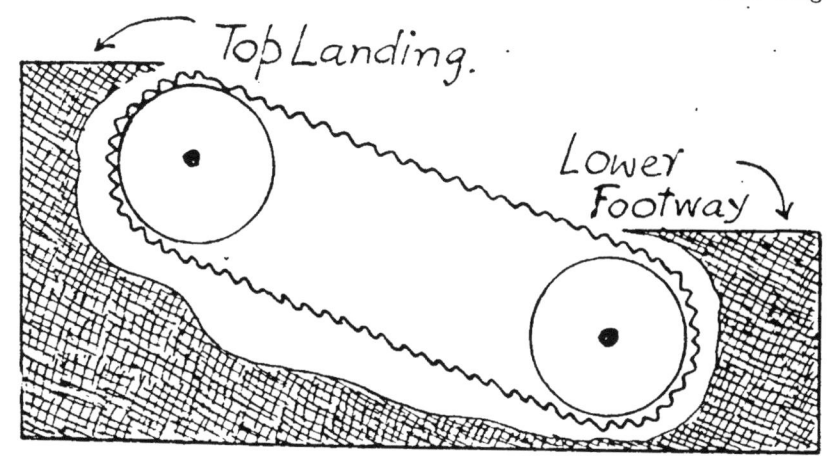

high and fairly narrow. Cut away the upper right-hand part; but shape the top landing and the lower footway by bending over sufficient of the sides to provide these platforms. Paste strips of paper along the edges where the cardboard needs joining.

The stairway is formed by a strip of corrugated paper. It figures as an endless belt, and therefore needs joining at the ends. To do this neatly, unstick the two thicknesses at both ends of the paper, and cut away a strip of the crinkled material from one and the flat material from the other; then lap the remaining two and so form the endless belt.

The belt revolves round two cotton reels. The upstanding flanges of these must be levelled by winding paper or cloth round them until the material reaches the height of the flanges. Then a piece of sheet rubber is wrapped round the reel and tied with cotton. If an old bicycle tube is handy, cut a piece just wide enough to slip on to the reel and cover it. When no rubber is available a piece of velvet will make a good substitute. The idea of using rubber or velvet is to prevent the belt slipping, as it will do when the reels are shod with some smooth material.

The reels having been attended to, a length of pencil is passed through both and wedged tightly. Each piece of pencil must be long enough to reach from one side of the box to the other and allow a part to project on either side.

At this point the belt is slipped round the two reels, which are held as far apart as possible. In this position they are placed beside the box, and the best angle to fit them is noted. The spot is marked where the pencils are to come, and then holes are cut to take them.

The reels and the belt are now put in the box, the sides of which are temporarily sprung out to permit of the proper fitting of the pencil ends.

On revolving the upper pencil, the escalator travels upwards, and when the lower pencil is revolved the staircase moves downwards. See that the upper and lower platforms are cut away sufficiently to let the band work properly, and if each reel is not quite as wide as the box place it centrally on the pencil shaft and run a sloping strip of cardboard along either side of the escalator and a trifle above it.

A TRAIN INDICATOR

The following makes an admirable plaything. If required for use with miniature scale railways it must be given proportions to harmonise with the other accessories; but otherwise it is best to make it on the large side, say four by three by one inch.

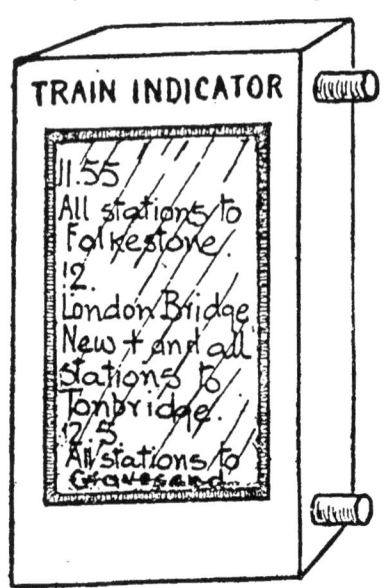

Hundreds of Things a Boy Can Make

The first thing is to secure a well-made cardboard box with these dimensions or to make the shape of stout card. Then to cut out a space three by one and a half inches from the bottom of the box, placing it equi-distant from sides as well as ends. See that the edges of the opening are neatly formed and not in any way jagged.

Next bore four circular holes in the narrow sides of the box, two on one edge and two on the other. They should be placed a trifle nearer the ends of the box than the short edges of the cut-out space. Place a small wooden roller horizontally through each pair of holes and let them project a quarter of an inch on the outside of the box.

Now take a strip of white calico, or thin but tough paper about a yard long and a quarter of an inch wider than the width of the opening in the box, and write on it such times and destinations as the following:

    11.55 All Stations to Folkestone.
    12.0   London Bridge, New Cross, and all Stations to Tonbridge.
    12.5   All Stations to Gravesend.
    12.10 Fast Train to Hastings.

Then fix one end of the strip to the upper and the other to the lower roller. Note that a short piece at each end of the strip should be left blank.

Lastly paint the sides of the box to resemble a train-indicator.

To use, twist the rollers and the indicating strip brings new times and destinations into view.

A CANNON THAT CAN BE FIRED

A cannon that can be fired will attract a good many boys. The diagram shows a first-rate model that can be put together in a very short while. A pair of wheels and a tube to take the ammunition must be obtained first, and the rest should be built around them.

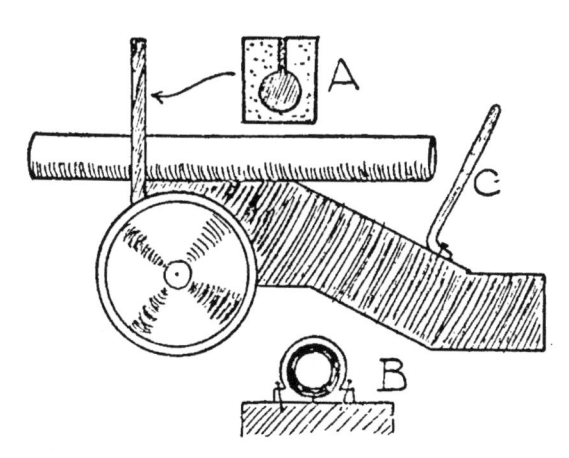

For the wheels, probably a pair that will serve quite well can be gleaned from a broken tin toy—you should never throw away wheels that are sound when the rest of a model is past use; they will come in sooner or later for something you want to make, and you will not have to buy a set.

The tube can be shaped out of a piece of iron piping, an unwanted pea-shooter, or even a length of pith cane.

The gun-carriage is a block of wood. If the shape is too difficult to cut in one piece, do it in two or even three sections and nail them together. The length of the carriage ought to be about three times the diameter of the selected wheels and the height a trifle more than the diameter of the wheels.

To make the model appear realistic a bullet-proof screen should be fitted to the fore-part of the carriage. This is cut out of wood a quarter of an inch thick and shaped as drawn in A. The circle, shown in the small picture, is a sectional view of the firing tube.

The tube is fixed to the gun-carriage by binding a strip of brass or tinned iron around it and nailing it down to the carriage. (See Diagram B.) Two of these strips are required to keep the parts together.

The firing apparatus consists of a piece of flexible metal (shown at C). A short length of the spring taken from a mechanical toy is just the thing for the purpose; but any strip of "springy" metal will serve. To operate the firing gear insert a short length of wooden rod that can pass through the tube easily; but leave a quarter of an inch of the rod projecting at the rear end. Then force back the metal arm at C and let it spring forward with a jerk.

The charge shoots out of the tube, and with a little practice it will not be difficult to hit any given mark that is within range. Note that the projectile should never be fired towards a person.

THE MUSICAL WINDMILL

The following small contrivance provides a nice little toy for your young brother or sister. It is a windmill which makes a musical sound, and, as you know, anything which causes a noise is appreciated by tiny folk.

First, get a piece of three-ply wood about six inches square, and smooth the edges nicely with a piece of glass paper. Then find the centre, and there rig up a little collar, about half an inch to an inch off the surface level. This is the hardest part of the construction, but it can be done in many ways. The easiest is to cut a bridge out of stout card-board and pierce the centre of the level stretch, then tack the horizontal sides to the board. A much better way is to obtain a strip of sheet zinc, and shape it as shown in the small diagram.

Step number two consists in fitting the stem of a cheap pen-holder in the circular opening of the zinc collar. It must not wobble in the collar, and the bottom end should be sharpened to a point so that it does not drag on the ground.

Step three is the fitting of six horizontal arms to the top of the pen-holder, on which are glued little wings of paper. Dead match sticks do well for the purpose.

All this being done, the next thing is to push a long stout pin through the pen-holder, just a little way above the supporting collar.

Now for the last step. Blow on the paper wings and merrily round will spin the pen-holder, taking with it the horizontal pin. Note the circumference described by the tip of the pin. A little within this circle, pencil a new circle and drive into it about fifty equi-distant tall pins. Now when the pen-holder is blown round, the horizontal pin strikes each upright pin and causes a musical sound. It will be quite easy to tune up the pins, so that the sounds are like going up and down the notes on a piano. This is done by forcing a pin in the wood, a little more or less than the pin next to it.

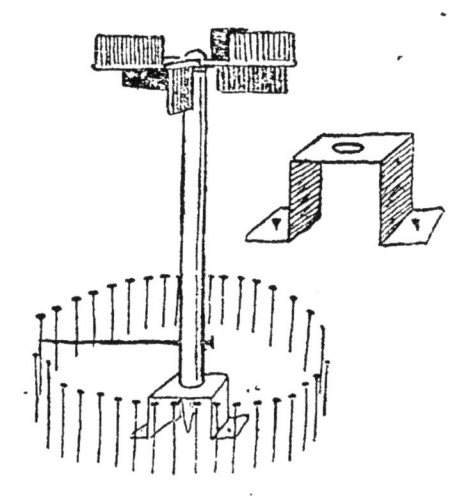

If you are clever at constructing things, it will not be a bad idea to make a stouter prop than here suggested, and instead of the horizontal pin, use a bit of a spring out of a broken mechanical toy. This will give much more sound, but you will also have to blow on the wings a good deal harder.

MODELS MADE OF CEMENT

Portland cement is not usually associated with the making of attractive toy models; nevertheless it offers a very useful means of constructing them. Let us suppose that you want a good strong bridge to form part of the lay-out of a model railway. Hardly anything could be suggested that would suit the purpose better than cement. It is cheap, easily worked, very strong, and when the first model has been made others can be constructed with great facility. Of course many things besides bridges can be produced in the manner described under this heading.

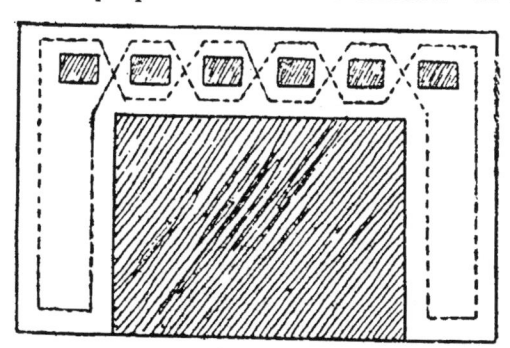

The first step is to draw a rough sketch of the model to be made, marking on it the exact dimensions of each part. We will suppose that the roadway of the bridge is to be six inches wide, eighteen inches long, and the extreme height from the ground to the road level is a foot. Start by making a box with these dimensions.

The next step is to cut blocks of wood to fill in the spaces where the bridge is open. Say, for instance, that each pillar is to be four inches wide. The two together come to eight inches, and as the total length of the model is eighteen inches, that will leave ten inches as the length between them. Therefore cut a block of wood ten inches long and as thick as the depth of the box, which is six inches. The roadway, we will say, is to be three inches deep. As the box is twelve inches, it leaves nine inches, and that must be the third dimension of the block. Having cut the wood, 10 × 6 × 9 inches, nail it to the box in its appropriate position.

Now look at the diagram. The large shaded area shows this block in position. The smaller shaded parts show further blocks of wood nailed to the bottom of the box and arranged equi-distant. They serve for ornamentation and will appear in the actual bridge as open spaces. Of course the design can be made more intricate, at will, by the addition of other wood blocks.

At this stage take some stout wire and bend it so that it runs round each piece of wood, without touching, and down to the foot of both pillars. Put it on one side for a few moments.

Next mix up some cement, using half a cupful of Portland cement and a full cup of fine red sand. Use just enough water to make it wet without being "sloppy." Mix the ingredients very thoroughly, then put it into the box-mould. See that the corners and edges are thoroughly filled and use an old table-knife for the purpose.

When the box has been covered all over to half of its thickness drop the wire shape into position, and then fill the box up to the top of its edges and smooth the surface quite level.

Now place the box in a dark cupboard, not near any warmth, and leave for some days to harden. The slower the hardening, the stronger will be the model.

After four or five days it should be possible to turn the cement bridge out of the box, and, if the latter is not damaged in the process, other bridges can be moulded in it.

Printed in Great Britain
by Amazon.co.uk, Ltd.,
Marston Gate.